CW00881677

THE PR   I
PROPERTY PUZZLE

**Discover the most expensive mistakes
London property buyers make and
how you can acquire your ideal home
on the best terms possible**

JEREMY McGIVERN

No part of this book may be reproduced in any form or by any electronic or mechanical means including information storage and retrieval systems, without permission in writing from the author. The only exception is by a reviewer, who may quote short excerpts in a published review.

The information presented herein represents the views of the author as of the date of publication. This book is presented for informational purposes only. Due to the rate at which conditions change, the author reserves the right to alter and update his opinions at any time. While every attempt has been made to verify the information in this book, the author does not assume any responsibility for errors, inaccuracies, or omissions.

ISBN: 978-07552-1527-0

© Jeremy McGivern 2012
All rights reserved

Contents

Preface

I wrote this book and I offer it to you because I saw a tremendous need for a practical, no-nonsense guide to buying property in prime central London.

As the founder and managing director of Mercury Homesearch, London's internationally renowned property search agency, I've been acquiring upscale properties for an elite list of clients since 2001. I've appeared on Bloomberg Televison and my opinions have been sought by *The Financial Times*, *The Times*, *The Sunday Times*, *The Daily Telegraph*, *Forbes Magazine*, *MoneyWeek* and numerous other major publications. I was also named as one of the most influential figures in Prime Central London property in Spears' Wealth Management's *Property Power Index*.

Why did I found a residential property consultancy?
Because I was deeply unhappy with the service and advice I was receiving as a buyer. I realised that the market was rigged against buyers and resolved to revolutionise how properties were bought in prime central London.

I bought my first home in 1996. My father had kindly given me and my brother (who was still at Edinburgh University) the deposit for a house. I lost count of the number of homes I viewed and how many our father rejected, but I remember my undiluted excitement when we bought a four bedroom house that later proved to be a fantastic home and investment. When my brother decided to get married we sold the house, as his wife strangely did not want to live in the same house as me!

I started looking for a new home, but the initial excitement turned to boredom, which then turned to frustration. I could not understand why the process of buying a home was so painful. Had the estate agents been this poor four years earlier? Why was I being shown completely inappropriate properties despite my requirements being very clear? (I did not realise it at the time, but of course the only thing that had changed was me). The process continued until I found what I considered to be an under-priced property, which I bought, refurbished, and sold for a substantial profit.

I repeated this process, but became increasingly perplexed by the estate agents. They knew me well by this stage, but were still showing me properties that they must have known I would never buy. It was then that I realised that the estate agents were not really interested in what I, the buyer, wanted. Their legal obligation was to sell their clients' property at the highest price, not to find me my ideal home. I also discovered that not only did they have sales targets to hit, but *viewing* targets as well, so my precious time was an irrelevance to them.

The birth of a club

On realising this I determined that there had to be a better way to acquire property in Prime Central London, so I founded Mercury Homesearch. The concept was, and still is, simple: to ensure that buyers acquire the finest property available on the best terms possible while making it an enjoyable and outstanding experience. This is achieved by using our proprietary processes – The Dominant Buyer System and The True Value Matrix.

Over ten years later:

- Having spoken to 232+ estate agents every week for over ten years (which means a minimum of 120,640 phone conversations);
- Having physically viewed over 22,000 properties in prime central London;
- Having studied the details of over 153,400 apartments, houses and investment opportunities (and rejected them as unsuitable);
- Having built up an unrivalled network of "off market" contacts;

I am widely acknowledged as being the leading expert on acquiring property in Prime Central London, especially Belgravia, Knightsbridge, Mayfair, the Royal Borough of Kensington and Chelsea, Marylebone and St James's.

The information in this book is relevant to anyone looking to acquire £1m+ properties in prime central London: Members of Mercury Homesearch have included families in the *Forbes* 100 as well as some of the world's leading CEOs and entrepreneurs. While just over thirty percent of our members are British and based in London, we also serve members from India, Italy, Dubai, Greece, Qatar, Brazil, America, France, New Zealand, Hong Kong, South Africa, Russia, Singapore, Georgia, The Philippines and Sweden.

Introduction

If you're planning to acquire a property in one of London's internationally renowned addresses, then you have one goal: to buy the finest property available on the best terms possible. In order to achieve this goal, you need to exercise the same care and attention you would when making any other major investment.

Unfortunately, because of the estate agent system, the London property market is biased against buyers. This is true whether you are born and bred in London or if you are based overseas. Consequently buyers literally throw away hundreds of thousands of pounds, and in some cases millions, by making one of seven basic mistakes.

Fortunately these mistakes can be extremely simple to avoid.

This report will show you how. Whether you are purchasing a house which will be your retreat from the frenetic pace of London life, whether you wish to find a home in which to entertain and amaze your friends, or whether you simply want a good investment, these strategies will help you find the best property in your criteria without wasting huge amounts of time and money, and experiencing unnecessary stress.

Throughout this report you will find testimonials from former clients and case studies. The purpose of these is not to sing our praises (although I admit it is nice to be recognised) but to prove that these strategies work and are absolutely necessary if you want to achieve the best terms possible. The problem is that some of the advice we suggest almost seems too simple. As someone once said (I apologise I can't remember who), "Successful people do the simple, easy-to-do things that unsuccessful people don't do because they don't recognise them as what really matters."

Please note that although confidentiality is essential for our members, they have kindly offered to give their names so that you can be certain that the comments are true and not a figment of my imagination!

A simple formula for successfully acquiring your ideal home
The information and strategies you are about to learn are the culmination of over a decade's experience buying property in prime central London combined with research we had conducted by an independent company, Empire Research Group.

I will show you the techniques we use to obtain "inside information" so that our clients can have first refusal on the most exquisite properties.

These are proven strategies that you can use to acquire distressed properties or the outstanding property in your criteria before other buyers have even heard about them. Just as importantly, you will discover how you can avoid throwing away vast sums of money unnecessarily.

Proof this works...

"We had been looking to acquire a property in Prime Central London for some time. We had asked various companies to help us with this, but were having little success. By chance we mentioned this to a business associate who recommended that I speak to their property adviser, Jeremy McGivern, at Mercury Homesearch. Within two weeks he had found two suitable properties. He provided detailed information on both properties and gave us objective advice...

It was a pleasure to deal with Jeremy and the whole process was extremely smooth. He was efficient and knowledgeable as one would expect. We continue to have him represent us and would highly recommend you employ his services if you wish to buy a property in London."

– For and on behalf of Enduring Overseas Inc., Knightsbridge

1. The Prime Central London Property Market

Prime Central London consists of a number of neighbourhoods including Knightsbridge, Belgravia, Mayfair, Kensington, Chelsea, and Notting Hill. Along these streets you'll find a stunning array of modern and classical architecture that attracts the most discerning buyers. For centuries, Eaton Square, Chester Square, Grosvenor Square, Egerton Crescent, and Park Lane have been internationally desirable addresses. More recent developments such as The Knightsbridge, One Hyde Park, and Montrose Place provide the finest contemporary facilities including spas, concierges, underground parking and twenty-four-hour security for those requiring a family apartment or London base without the concerns of maintenance and other issues that may be associated with classical buildings.

The market can be very competitive, and buyers can make some hugely expensive mistakes when acquiring luxury properties. Although the Prime Central London property market is mature, the estate agent system creates a bias against buyers. But if you understand how the London property market works, then you can use the system to your advantage.

Although it is incredibly obvious, very few buyers realise that they are at a disadvantage. This is because of the status quo – the way buying and selling property in

London has been handled for centuries. A decade ago many assumed that with the advent of the Internet and property websites the situation would improve. In fact this has probably led to many buyers becoming more complacent and even less thorough in their search.

In fact, research by *The Financial Times* has discovered that the average buyer only spends ninety-six minutes viewing properties before they buy. This is forty-three minutes less than people typically spend deciding on where to go on holiday or which computer to buy. If you follow the same strategy, the probability of your finding the best property available is extremely low. In fact, relying on the Internet could prove disastrous, as you will learn later.

When buying property in Prime Central London, the Two Percent Rule definitely applies: Ninety-eight percent of buyers do the same thing and so buy poor or average properties. Two percent make good deals and acquire real value.

When you are spending millions of pounds on a property, going along with the herd simply isn't an option.

Fortunately for you, you can be one of the two percent who turns this situation to your benefit.

Why are buyers at a disadvantage?
The reason is simple: estate agents. The majority of property in London is sold through estate agents. This is hardly a revelation. The problem is that most buyers forget the real role of the agents.

It is essential that you remember the following:

- Estate agents are employed by owners. They are legally obliged to sell their clients' property for the highest price possible, on the most favourable terms possible. They only have a "thin legal duty" to buyers.
- You are not the priority. Each agent can have over one hundred buyers registered with him or her. As friendly as the agents may be, they are not concerned who buys the property as long as a high price is achieved for their client. Their focus is not to find you your perfect home, but to sell one of their clients' properties to you.
- Each estate agent can only show you a small percentage of the properties available. The agents can only show you the properties on which they have been directly instructed. Therefore you need to be registered with every suitable agent to ensure that you do not miss out on the best opportunities. (It is true that some properties are shared amongst the agents. However, these tend to be the properties that they are having trouble selling).
- The finest properties in Prime Central London rarely reach the open market. You need to be able to source those exclusive "off market" properties that the average homebuyer never even knows exists.

Estate agents are often listed in the top ten least popular professions because buyers forget the agents' real role. However, many estate agents are extremely good. As a seller that is great news, but obviously poses challenges for you.

This is why acquiring a home is rarely the enjoyable, exciting experience that it should be. If you employ the same approach as the typical buyer, you will find it an unbelievably time consuming and frustrating battle.

Of course, if you are based outside of London or are simply extremely busy, the problems are exacerbated: it is harder to discover all the relevant agents and to stay in regular contact. In addition it will also be very difficult to view properties. Therefore the estate agents are more likely to contact other buyers about the best properties before they call you. It is a simple fact that they will be more likely to earn their commission by focussing on clients who are easy to contact and can view properties quickly.

If you are similar to our clients, you are highly successful and either focussing on business opportunities or other interests. However, you must find the time to carry out the necessary research to find the finest property in your criteria and ensure that you are not paying an excessive price. Most buyers fail to plan their acquisition. Therefore they actually spend more time than is necessary, fail to find the best properties, and end up making an average purchase at a high price.

Fortunately, you can avoid these issues by following a few simple steps to ensure that you make an astute acquisition.

2. Preparation – The Simplest Way to Save Time, Money and Stress

I'm not going to pretend that the process of preparation and planning is exciting. In fact it is remarkably dull, which is why most buyers fail to undertake this most basic and important step. However, the results will be exceptional and the good news is that you can delegate most of the work.

Fortunately for you, most buyers do not treat the purchase of a home as a business transaction. Consequently they are ill prepared. You must not make the same mistake.

Why must you be prepared? So that you will be in a position to act swiftly when you find your perfect home. If you are not, then it is likely that you will suffer the frustration of losing it to another buyer. We have also often been able to secure advantageous terms for our clients or had offers accepted which were not the highest put forward, simply because we made sure we were able to act more quickly than anyone else.

One classic example was a building we acquired for a client in Kensington in 2009. The property comprised of three flats, which the owners had planned to convert back to a house. The attraction of the building was that it included the original artist's studio with fantastic light and double height rooms (their plans to develop the property would have ruined this, but that is another story). However, we had discovered that the owners had got themselves into serious financial trouble and needed to sell quickly. We were able to secure the property at a very favourable price simply because we had ensured that our clients were fully prepared for such an eventuality and could exchange contracts in three days.

You can do the same with some very basic preparation:

- Have your finances in place. However you plan to finance the acquisition, you have to ensure your financier is aware of your plans so that he or she can move quickly when asked. As a rule, you will need to put down five to ten percent of the purchase price as a deposit on the exchange of contracts. The balance is paid upon completion. It is possible, although rare, to exchange within hours of seeing a property.

   If you require a mortgage or financing, it is essential that this is agreed in principle before you start looking and that you have a broker who can organise swift approval of the mortgage when it is required.

- Have the correct tax structure in place. For non-UK residents this is absolutely essential. It is vital that you have a team of advisors who understand the necessary tax structures.

   You must have this organised prior to making an offer, otherwise there will be delays. Any unnecessary delays may cause you to lose the property. The vendor can pull out of the agreement at any time, especially if the transaction is taking too long. Remember, the agreement is not legally binding until contracts have been exchanged. Why take this risk?

- Prepare for Stamp Duty Land Tax (SDLT). This is payable by the buyer on the purchase of a property. It is currently 6% for transactions over £1 million and 7% for properties over £2m. It may be possible for you to avoid paying this although many solicitors do not offer advice on this. This is simply because it is not their area of expertise. Therefore it is essential that you choose your solicitor carefully.

- Instruct a solicitor. It is essential that you use a solicitor who specialises in London property transactions. You would not rely on a criminal expert to work on a corporate case, so do not instruct a solicitor who is not a property ("conveyancing" is the technical term) specialist. Again they must be available to act as soon as you are ready to make a purchase. Therefore, you should have instructed a solicitor to act for you before you even start looking for a property.

  There are money laundering laws which require solicitors to check identifications and the source of funds before a transaction can proceed. This will be more complicated if a specialist structure is being used. Have everything in place so that you can avoid unnecessary delays.

- Instruct a surveyor. In most cases a survey will need

to be carried out. You need to have two or three surveyors prepared to act for you at short notice.

- Be available. You may need to view properties at short notice. Obviously this may not always be possible, but if you have people whose opinion you trust, ask them to view properties for you.

If you are well prepared this will be the basic foundation for your success. If you are not, I can guarantee you will have to endure one of the following three scenarios. You will:

1. Miss the best opportunities. Our best acquisitions have always been made when we have been able to move swiftly and pre-empt other buyers.

2. Have to offer more to make your bid more attractive than that of another buyer who can move more quickly than you.

3. Lose the property even if you have agreed a price and been sent the contract. The delays caused by your lack of preparation will mean the seller will lose confidence in your ability to complete the purchase. They will allow other potential buyers to acquire the property. You will have wasted a lot of time, energy and money.

Important note: Property transactions are often complicated and can take time. There is no legally binding agreement until you have exchanged contracts. Agreeing on the price is *not* the end of the negotiation and is *not* legally binding.

How to avoid wasting time

The main reason why buyers waste huge amounts of time is that they are not truly focussed on what they want. When we first meet our clients we spend considerable time discussing their requirements to ensure that everything has been considered.

It is essential that you refine your criteria so that you have a clearly defined picture of what you require. If you do not, you will spend hours looking at unsuitable properties.

You obviously need to know the basics like the number of bedrooms, bathrooms, whether you need a separate dining room, budget, etc. However, you also need to consider:

- House or flat?
- Location and access to transport/parking for cars
- Access to shops, galleries, theatre
- The condition of the property
- Architectural styles – both internal and external
- How many bedrooms?
- How many bathrooms? How many ensuite?
- Length of lease
- Will you require a lift?
- Views and orientation
- Service charges
- Will you require a garage, swimming pool, gym, media room, etc?
- How important is a porter, concierge or caretaker?
- Do you need a guest loo?

- Terraced, semi-detached, detached?
- Garden, patio, roof terrace/balcony?
- Family kitchen or galley kitchen?
- Dining room/office/play room
- Pet/child friendly
- Which floor/On how many floors?

We have discovered that one of the most revealing questions we ask is: "What do you want to *avoid*?" By answering this question you'll paint a clearer picture of what you *want* and therefore reduce the amount of time wasted on viewing unsuitable properties.

You will also quickly be able to assess whether your criteria are realistic and modify them accordingly. Too many buyers spend months trying to find "a needle in a haystack" when in fact the needle never existed in the first place.

If buying an investment property, be very clear on what returns you require. Do not make the mistake of confusing your criteria – just because *you* would not live in a certain area or type of property does not make it a bad investment.

Proof this works...

"We used Mercury to help us find an investment property in London. We were not going to have time to evaluate the market fully ourselves and wanted someone to give us good, honest advice on location and value, and to find us the best property that would meet our objectives. They did just that. They were also extremely efficient and helpful, not only up to completion but also afterwards. We would use them again."

– Mr. C. Dowling (Chelsea & Kensington)

3. A Brief Overview of Leasehold Properties

By Tim Martin at Marr-Johnson & Stevens

If you are not British the concept of a lease may seem strange if not downright foolish. However, if you understand your legal rights then there is nothing to fear.

Leases as a form of tenure

Buyers of most flats (and some houses) in central London will find that they are held on leases. They are called leasehold properties. In the UK, we use the term "freehold" to describe properties that are owned outright with no defined period of ownership.

Fundamentally, a lease is a contract that permits the leaseholder to occupy and control the property for a specified number of years, at the end of which it reverts back to the landlord. On the face of it this might seem an unattractive form of tenure, but well informed buyers will also know that it holds significant advantages too.

It stands to reason that a shorter lease will be less valuable than a longer one, and this means that there can be a wide variety of prices for properties in the same area which are, in all other respects, virtually identical. For buyers who are unwilling or unable to commit the full price to a property immediately, this has an obvious advantage.

Allied to this, normally after two years of ownership, a buyer will become eligible to acquire the freehold of his house, or an extension of the lease of his flat. This enables him to acquire his property in two stages, the latter stage at a time almost entirely of his own choosing, and this gives him great flexibility. It is usually also possible for a group of flat owners to get together to buy the freehold of their block, and this can be done immediately. However, it should be noted that some leases cannot be extended; broadly, if the term at the start of the lease was for more than twenty-one years, the lease is a qualifying lease. If it is not then you need to make enquiries.

The terms of a lease

Being a contract, a lease is inevitably a more complex form of tenure than freehold ownership, and it will contain various rights and obligations, of which the more important ones include:

- Ground rent. Most leases will require the tenant to pay an annual ground rent to the landlord. This can be anything from a few pounds per year to many thousands. Some leases permit the landlord to review or increase the rent, either by fixed amounts or by reference to other formulae, and care must be taken by buyers and their advisers in checking the rental provisions in the lease.
- Repairs and service charges. The lease will set out who is responsible for keeping the property in repair. Generally, the tenant of a flat is responsible for main-

taining and repairing the interior of the flat, and the landlord is responsible for maintenance and repair of the block, including any lifts, common parts, the provision of porterage, etc. The landlord is usually entitled to recover its costs from the tenants by means of a service charge, which is raised regularly throughout each year. It is a fact that well maintained blocks usually have higher service charges, but the corollary is that the flats in such blocks retain their value much better than those in less well run buildings.

- Alterations. A buyer will often want to carry out works to the flat, ranging from a simple redecoration to a complete refurbishment, possibly including structural changes. Leases often permit minor non-structural works, but there are tighter controls on major works, particularly if they involve structural alterations. In almost all cases, the landlord's consent will be needed for all but the most minor works, but that consent usually cannot be unreasonably withheld. Sometimes the prohibition can be absolute, but in practice, this is used as a means of exercising greater control, not as a way of preventing any works at all. Given the wide variation on the possible controls that might be found in it, it is always sensible to read the lease before undertaking any works.

- Selling and underletting. If a tenant wants to sell his property, known as assigning the lease, the landlord's consent will often be required, but that consent usually cannot be withheld or delayed. Likewise, leases often contain controls over letting the flat out, and the landlord's consent is normally required as well. In both instances, it is normal for the tenant to have to register the changes with the landlord, and a small fee is often payable for the service.

- Use. Most leases prohibit business use and, instead, require the flat to be used for residential purposes only. As ever, what constitutes business use is often open to interpretation. For example, a landlord is unlikely to try and stop a tenant from using part of the flat for occasional work, but they probably would stop a tenant from using it on an everyday basis as a fully operational office. And of course it's virtually impossible to know whether a tenant is using the flat for an internet business that requires no foot traffic or deliveries.

- Extending the lease or buying the freehold. Although becoming eligible to acquire the freehold or an extended lease is straightforward, the process itself is less so. While this should be no reason to be put off from buying a leasehold property, it does require specialist advice from lawyers and valuers who should have a demonstrable track record of carrying out this work.

Obtaining proper advice about the likely cost of acquiring the freehold or extended lease is an important tool for a buyer to check whether he is paying the correct amount for the lease. Generally, the market now prices leases by first assessing what the property would be worth freehold (or on a very long lease as the case may be) and then deducting the cost of acquiring the freehold or extended lease. The balance represents the maximum amount that can be spent on buying the normal or short lease. Clearly, an error in either of these components will lead to an error in pricing the short lease.

4. How to Become a Preferred Buyer, and Why Websites Are Dangerous

I've already mentioned this, but it is worth repeating. The majority of properties are sold through estate agents, which puts buyers at a disadvantage. Here's why.

- Estate agents are employed by owners. They are legally obliged to sell their clients' property for the highest price possible and on the most favourable terms possible.
- You are not the priority. Each agent can have over one hundred buyers registered with him or her. As friendly as the agents may be, they are not concerned who buys the property as long as a full price is achieved for their client. Their focus is not to find you your perfect home, but to sell one of their clients' properties to you.

This does not mean that you should avoid the agents. One of the biggest mistakes that buyers make is insisting on only seeing "off market" properties. This is partly because they are in contact with the bigger agents and therefore assume, wrongly, that they are seeing everything openly available. There is also the view that "off market" properties are more prestigious. Indeed this can be the case.

Nevertheless, the agents will be your main source of properties. However, you cannot rely on them to contact you. You need to ensure that you are at the top of their list of "preferred buyers." This will be essential as you want to be the first to hear about the best opportunities when they become available. Therefore you need to:

- Register with every estate agent in your target area. Remember the agents can only show you the properties on which they have been directly instructed. Therefore you need to be registered with every suitable agent to ensure that you do not miss out on the best opportunities. At the time of writing there are 223 estate agencies in Prime Central London. If you only register with ten agents you are immediately reducing the probability and likelihood of success.

- Do not rely on the Internet. Because it seems like the most efficient way to source properties in such a fragmented market, over seventy-five percent of people start their search online. Unfortunately, they are severely hindering their chances of seeing the best properties. This is because the best property that comes to the market often sells before going onto the Internet. Indeed Savills reported that 46% of properties on its books at £2+ million are *only* available privately, and Knight Frank reports more than thirty percent of sales of £2+ million homes and fifty-two percent of the £5+ million are off-market properties.

- To be the first to see the best properties, you must contact the agents at least once a week.
- Provide a clear list of criteria for the estate agents and they will see that you are serious and focussed on the search. The clearer the requirements the less of your time will be wasted. However, you have to strike a balance; be careful not to be too exact otherwise the agents may omit to tell you about suitable properties.
- Let the agents know you are in a position to move quickly and that you are well organised. Ultimately they want any sale to go through quickly and easily so that they can earn their commission. Show them that you are prepared and will act professionally.
- Build a good relationship with the agents. Call them at least once a week and do not rely on email, which is impersonal and will be deleted and forgotten.
- View properties whenever possible or have a representative view them on your behalf. However, if you do not think a property is worth viewing explain why to the agent, so that he or she gets a better picture of what you want.
- The day after a viewing, give feedback on the property. Very few people do this and it will make you stand out.

Of course, if you are based overseas, you must be careful not to constantly call the agents if you know you are not going to be in London to view the properties. The agents may begin to think that you are wasting their time. They make their living by selling properties, so will understandably focus on those buyers who are actively looking, and will not be motivated to call when you actually are ready to view. So you need to judge how often you should call them – perhaps just call twice a month for updates until a month before you arrive in London. Then follow the steps outlined above.

Again this advice may seem simple, but too many buyers rely on websites and email hoping that technology will make life easier. It is easier, but not effective. If everyone else is doing this how do you expect to gain an advantage and have first refusal on the best properties?

5. How to Spot the Best Opportunities

I find this an extraordinary fact, but according to research carried out by the *Daily Telegraph* the average property buyer spends just ninety-six minutes in total viewing potential properties before they buy. This is forty-six minutes less than people typically spend choosing a holiday or buying a computer.

Needless to say this is not an intelligent approach to acquiring a multi-million-pound asset and explains why nearly half of all buyers experience a problem ranging from noise pollution to unpleasant neighbours to structural problems. Consequently you need to have a standard plan for each viewing, so that you consider all the possible issues. This is especially important because it is very easy to be attracted to a property because of the stunning façade or beautiful artwork and furnishings inside, which can distract you from issues which are not immediately noticeable but could be hugely problematic. A classic example of this is airplane noise; parts of Chelsea are directly under the flight path to Heathrow, which will obviously have repercussions if you are a light sleeper and the building does not allow air-conditioning and/or double glazing.

You need to have a plan in place that should include the following:

Do not always dismiss a property before you have

nitially it is worth seeing as many properties
o get a feel for what is available and to make
ven't inadvertently discounted a potential
ᵤ ᵢ. ᵤf property. You will also quickly learn how to
read between the lines of the agents' details.

Question the agents before you view. Don't blindly
believe the agents or the details they send you. Remember
that the agent is employed to sell their client's house. You
are not the priority. The best way to avoid the frustration
of pointless viewings is to ask a few questions to find out
if the property at least meets your basic criteria.

Always be polite and punctual. The agent may not be,
but this is business and you want them to be on your
side. Also try to be flexible on viewing times and do not
repeatedly cancel, because this will give the impression
you are not serious.

Ask pertinent questions. The length of time the property has been on the market will be more useful
information for the negotiation than the age of the
boiler. The more information you have for the negotiations the better. Good questions to ask are:

- Why is the owner selling?
- How long has the property been on the market?
- How many viewings have there been?
- How many offers have you had?
- When does the vendor need to move?
- What is the minimum price the seller will accept?
- What do you think the property will sell for?
- Who priced the property?

- How many agents valued the property? Who valued it at what price?
- What other homes are there in competition with this property?
- Why do you think it hasn't sold yet?
- How quickly does the seller need to move?
- Where is the vendor moving to? Have they found anywhere?

Don't judge a book by its cover or its contents. Look past the hideous garden, peeling paint and curious furniture to see if the property suits your needs. A property can often seem smaller than it is simply because of the number of people or the amount of furniture in it. Try to imagine what it will be like once you have decorated and furnished the property to your tastes. Conversely, don't be swayed by the "developer's finish" or the smell of fresh bread that they just happen to be baking.

Check the curtains. This sounds ridiculous at first, but I am serious. Many rooms are made to look dark and dreary by oversized curtains even if the décor is quite light. This can give the impression that the house is dingy. Sometimes you can uncover a gem simply by removing the curtains altogether. We once acquired a great house for a client that had been on the market for ages because people thought that the main rooms were dark. The problem was heavy curtains coupled with lime coloured suede walls, which was an easy problem to fix.

Always take your list of criteria on viewings and always take notes. These will be invaluable when comparing properties you have seen. It is also advisable to take a notebook and tape measure with you because the agents may not always bring the details with them.

Maintain a poker face. Ask anyone accompanying you to do the same. If you enthuse about a property in front of the vendor or estate agent, it will make the negotiations harder. However, you must still continue to build rapport with the agent and the seller (if he or she is present) as this will help in the negotiations.

View the property at different times of day. It is always wise to view a property more than once and it will give you a chance to get a better feel for the surrounding area too. Walk around the neighbouring streets to make sure you feel comfortable in the area. See how many buildings are vacant or appear to be in poor condition. Always look at neighbouring properties to see if they are well kept. If not, enquiries should be made.

Stay in the property for at least ten minutes. You must check for noise, including the periodic rumble of trains or the roar of jets. Ask the agent if the property is tube-affected, but also listen out for noise from neighbours. This is especially important in older buildings that have been converted into apartments as the soundproofing to the apartment above can be extremely poor to non-existent. Therefore it is often wise to view these in the evening after work.

Speak to the neighbours. Make contact and simply ask,

"We're thinking about buying in the area. Do you enjoy living here and is there anything we should be aware of?" Most people are happy to answer these questions and they may know about a local planning issue, etc. that may have an impact. At the same time you'll be able to judge whether you would want to have them as your neighbour. (If you're not comfortable approaching the neighbours yourself, have someone pretend to be a potential buyer in the area and do this for you).

Always get the "particulars." While there will be times when there are no details, such as if the property is being sold discreetly, the agent should bring the details to the viewing. If he doesn't then you must insist that he emails or sends them to you. They will form part of your database later in the process when you are trying to establish value. Therefore you need to pay close attention even to the properties that are completely wrong for you. Do not treat these as wasted viewings but part of your knowledge building and data collecting.

Again, these ideas may seem simple but the facts do not lie: Nearly half of all buyers have problems with their homes after they buy. Conversely, we have bought exceptional homes and investments for clients because other buyers had not been able to see past cosmetic issues and see the true potential of the property.

A great example of this was a house we acquired in a prime street in Notting Hill. It had been on the market for nine months. It was an excellent house but originally had been slightly overpriced at £5.25 million. After five months the seller and estate agents had reduced the price to £4.5 million, but still no-one was buying despite the fact that the price was very reasonable – £4.75m would have been fair value in our opinion - and prices were increasing rapidly because the number of buyers far exceeded the supply of property. During this time we agreed to represent a client whose requirements were a close match for the house. The client questioned why what seemed to be such a good house at such a reasonable price was not selling. Our view was first, potential buyers were being put off simply by the fact that no-one else was bidding. The perception was that there must be something intrinsically wrong with the house, which was the same question our client was posing. Secondly, some of the décor was rather garish – the agents had advised the seller to repaint the house but he was convinced he had exceptional taste. It was clear that these two circumstances combined were putting off buyers.

We had two builders quote for the necessary redecoration, which eventually cost £30,000. We were then able to negotiate a further £130,000 reduction to the asking price.

6. Sourcing Off-Market Properties

London's finest and most exceptional homes rarely reach the open market. Obviously we have an advantage when sourcing these, because we have cultivated a vast network of over four hundred contacts, and we have an intimate knowledge of the finest properties in London. Therefore we are able to identify suitable homes for our members and can approach the owners directly.

Many homeowners approach us directly to enquire if their home would be appropriate for one of our clients. By doing so, they can sell their homes discreetly and be assured of a smooth and professionally handled transaction.

However, there are other strategies we employ which you can use too.

1. Place adverts in suitable publications like the *Financial Times* describing the type of property you require. Remember you need to attract the readers' attention, so make sure the headline stands out and make sure you position yourself as a strong buyer. This can be an expensive way to find a property as you may have to place numerous advertisements and are not guaranteed success.

2. If you have a very specific area you are targeting, walk the streets to identify potential properties and write a letter to the owners. The letter must emphasise

your strengths as a buyer and will be more likely to receive a response if you can discover the name of the owners from the electoral role or other sources. Letters addressed to the "homeowner" are more likely to be throw away before they are opened.

3. If you are looking for a property with a concierge or porter, visit suitable buildings and speak to them. Porters are a great source of information and if incentivised can ensure you hear about upcoming sales before they reach the market.

4. Contact developers directly. They may be happy to sell to you instead of placing the property on the open market for a number of reasons – they will save on marketing costs or an early sale might help their cashflow.

5. Inform friends and family that you are looking for a property. Many of our members require complete discretion, so this approach may not be suitable for you. However, if this is not an issue you may be surprised how often a friend of a friend or even a business acquaintance will know someone who is considering selling a property.

Unfortunately, if you have to make the initial approach, buying off-market property can put you in a weak position when negotiating. If the owners had not planned to move you may have to pay a premium to acquire the property. For some people this is irrelevant, as they only want the home of their dreams and the best of the best. However, if you are a skilled negotiator you should be able to counter this problem.

7. The Biggest Mistake You Can Make

I am often asked what is the biggest discount I have negotiated on a property. Unfortunately, this misses the point completely. The size of the discount is only relevant if the property is fairly valued. Negotiating a discount of twenty percent is no good if the property was fifty percent overvalued in the first place.

As an example, I was negotiating on a property that was on the market at £6 million. If I had not known the real value and if I had believed that a twenty-five per-cent discount (i.e. a purchase price of £4.5 million) represented a brilliant piece of negotiating, then my client would have overpaid by roughly £1 million.

If you want to make an astute acquisition, accurate information is essential. If you have a good feel for values then you will spot the bargains and be able to move before anyone else. You will also avoid unwittingly overpaying.

Unbelievably, people spend very little time doing the necessary research or calculations. Consequently buyers needlessly waste hundreds of thousands of pounds – and often considerably more – when a few hours of research was all that was required.

I am not suggesting that the price you calculate will be the price that you pay. There are some people who simply want to secure a home and will pay a premium to have it withdrawn from the market quickly. Conversely, others will want to ensure that they are achieving a very competitive price.

Ultimately that choice is down to the individual concerned. What you want, though, is to be able to make an informed decision.

Although we advise our clients on price, we also back up our valuations with accurate information. We have a huge database of recently sold properties that includes floorplans and detailed information on each property.

Unfortunately, accurate comparable data is not easy for the average buyer to obtain. The data is invariably incomplete and therefore dangerously misleading.

Remember the estate agent is paid by the seller to obtain the best terms possible. Therefore he is likely to give you comparables that enhance *their* position. *These may not be the best comparables!*

The Land Registry (www.landregistryonline.gov.uk) lists most transactions, so that you can see what properties have sold for in any given street. Unfortunately there is no information on the property other than price. (www.nethouseprices.com will also give you this information for free.)

The problem is that no two properties are the same even if they are in the same stucco fronted terrace in Belgravia. They could be configured differently, be a different size (because one has had an extension which is not obvious from the street) or the condition of the properties could be different. This makes the information provided by these sites nearly useless unless you have seen the comparable property yourself or at least have been able to look at the full details including the floorplan.

Therefore you will need to find your information from elsewhere.

The best sources will be:

- The properties you have seen, especially those that have sold. If you have conducted a thorough search over a period of a few months you should have seen numerous comparable properties. You should have kept all the details and made notes while viewing the properties, even if they were unsuitable. These will give you an excellent frame of reference. Invariably some of these homes will have been sold or reduced in price. Call all the relevant agents to see what they sold for and glean as much information as possible – e.g. did the agent think this was a good price for the seller? If yes, what did he think the property should have sold for? On what is he basing this valuation?

- What is available for sale? You will hopefully have seen all the comparable properties in your target area. However, there is an outside chance that you might find a property you like during your first two or three viewings. It is essential that you check that there is nothing better available. If you have only seen ten or twelve properties, you have probably only seen a small percentage of the market. Therefore the chances of you having seen the best property available are slim. You must call all the other agents to see if they have anything suitable or comparable. At the very least download details from websites like www.primelocation.com and www.globrix.com, or any of the other websites, so you can compare prices.

You can make offers on multiple properties simultaneously. Do not feel you have to handle one negotiation at a time. Therefore it makes sense to ensure you have seen all suitable properties available.

- Information from the estate agents. Ask other agents if they have recently sold a similar property to the one you like. If so, say you are trying to get a feel for the area and ask them to send the old details. Also see if they have anything similar at the moment. In some cases you may want to ask their opinion on the property in which you are interested. However, you need to take any opinions with a pinch of salt. If another agent gives his or her opinion, ask which properties they are using as comparables to form their opinion. Also ask the agents selling the property to justify the valuation. Ask them to provide comparable data. If they can't, quite often an agent will admit that a property is overvalued (to be fair to the agents, owners sometimes insist on asking for an inflated price despite the agents' advice). The more questions you ask, the more likely the agent might let slip a useful piece of information. Of course this needs to be a conversation rather than an inquisition.

Once you have collated all the data you must compare like for like.

It sounds obvious, but this is not always easy as prices can vary massively in the same street for one reason or another. Indeed they can vary in the same building. For example, a first floor apartment in a stucco fronted conversion will generally be more expensive per square foot than a top floor apartment in the same building. However, apartments on the higher floors in a modern building will be more expensive than those on lower floors.

Therefore you must be very careful as to what you use for comparables. Double check all information and find as many comparables as possible. Only once you have a good idea of what similar properties have sold for can you start making an informed decision on what you should be offering to acquire the property.

Points to consider when making your valuation

How does the price compare per square foot to similar homes in the area? This should only be used as a rough guide as there are many other factors to take into consideration.

How long is the lease in comparison to the comparables you are using?

How does the property differ to the comparables you are using? Does it have a lift? Is the condition better? Is there parking? Is there a garden or terrace? Is the other property affected by the tube? How will these differences affect the price?

How strong is the market? Is the market racing

up or is it stabilising before further falls? You cannot tell for certain, but you need to assess the state of the market.

How many similar properties are available? Is there an oversupply?

How many comparables do you have? If you only have one or two, you need to be very careful. It is possible that that purchaser paid a huge premium and so the price may not be a true indication of fair value. Conversely the buyer may have negotiated an extremely good price, so you may be put off making an offer because the property you like seems overpriced in comparison when in fact it may still be a good buy.

What makes this property stand out for you? It is essential to consider the value of the property to you rather than just the price.

The most important information is often related to the owners of the property themselves. Some useful questions to ask the agents and the owners include:

- How long has the property been on the market?
- How many viewings have you done in that time?
- How many offers have you had?
- Why do you think you have not had any offers?
- How did you calculate the asking price?
- What price do you think they would accept?
- Why are they selling?
- Where are they moving to and have they found somewhere to buy?
- What have they said about the lack of offers?

The better the relationship you have with the agent, the more information you will uncover and they may let slip a vital detail. This could make all the difference in the negotiation.

There are properties in prime central London for which there are no direct comparables. They are unique and command a premium for being so. These properties often do not reach the open market so the judgement on value will be very personal. I know of a house in Kensington where the owner had quietly let it be known that he would sell for £250 million. In these situations valuation is as much an art as a science, and negotiation skills are more important than ever. Whatever the property you wish to buy, you must decide on the maximum figure you would be happy to pay for the property. This must be decided *before* you start negotiating. This must also be a figure that you will commit to not exceeding as this will be the target for your negotiation.

An important note on short leases
Because they do not understand the leasehold system and/or believe short leases to be inherently bad, many buyers are put off acquiring short leases. Nevertheless, short leases can be very good acquisitions. However, this is a highly specialised field – some leases cannot be extended and valuing short leases and calculating the cost of the lease extension is extremely complicated. This is not something you should attempt yourself.

EATON SQUARE

CITY OF WESTMINS

8. Beginning the Negotiations

Proof this works...

"I have never had a service that I would recommend as whole-heartedly as Mercury Homesearch. From beginning to end, Mercury helped us through the tortuous process that is buying a house – from dealing with estate agents, to employing solicitors, negotiating the price (and getting a much better deal than I would have attempted) ... We'll be using them again."
– Mr & Mrs D. Loehnis (Lancaster Gate)

"We were extremely happy with Mercury's help... They provided us with background information... and gave us a very good sense of how realistically priced a property was... more importantly they turned out to be fantastic negotiators as well!"
– Mr M. Gwynne

There are only a few lucky people born in life with the natural ability to negotiate with skill and ease, who never seem to break a sweat or betray a single stray emotion, and who are able to persuade others to agree to what they want despite a perceived conflict of interest. They are rare, but they do exist. Make no mistake, however; these skills can be taught and learned. It's a misconception to think that only natural negotiators can ever be great negotiators. In fact you do not even need to be a great negotiator. To have a huge advantage, you only need to be slightly better than the majority of people. In order to gain this advantage, you simply have to learn some basic theories, strategies and tactics, which we will discuss here in greater detail.

Being able to negotiate well is a great advantage in many areas of life, whether you are acquiring a home, buying a car, or simply trying to put the children to bed. The strategies and techniques you will learn here can be applied to any situation, and once you have learned and practised them they will simply become second nature. The examples we use here focus on property negotiation for ease and clarity.

Remember, learning how to negotiate well is not unethical or unfair. Negotiation is a fundamental part of many business exchanges; it is simply a discussion aimed at reaching an agreement that is acceptable to both sides. Ideally, both parties should be relatively happy with the outcome. As you will learn, successful negotiation is not about bending people to your will, bludgeoning them into submission, or attempting to create a win-lose situation. There is always a sliding scale of success in every negotiation and, as you will learn, in the ideal scenario the opposition will always think they have "won." This does not mean that you should deliberately mislead them into making a bad decision, but neither does it mean that you should make unnecessary concessions to keep them happy.

It should be stressed that the skills and techniques you will learn here are not a magical fix even though you will be amazed at how simple and effective they are. The strategies you will learn will not guarantee that you agree every negotiation. In fact the only thing you can be sure of is that you will never successfully complete one hundred percent of your negotiations. Sometimes you will have to walk away from a property because you are unable to agree terms. Sometimes your children will insist on coming back downstairs to tell you that you haven't hugged them goodnight even though you already have twenty times (you may have guessed that I have two young children who are brutal negotiators themselves because they refuse to take "no" as an answer). However, by incorporating these strategies into any negotiation the probability of reaching a favourable outcome is greatly enhanced. Over time you will save yourself hundreds of thousands if not millions in business and other transactions as well as finding better solutions to negotiations you may have in your personal life.

You will also be surprised by just how often you have recourse to the techniques, and how much easier life becomes once you have learned to be a better negotiator.

A definition and explanation

The Oxford Dictionary of English defines negotiation as "discussion aimed at reaching an agreement." But how many people enter a negotiation genuinely seeking an agreement? I would suggest a very small percentage. In fact most people approach the negotiation from the very narrow perspective of "trying to get the result I want." Obviously this is an important objective to achieve, but if you are solely focussed on this then you are severely limiting your chances of success. Why? Because there are a minimum of two sides to any negotiation. Therefore you need to consider the wishes and emotions of the other side(s) to give yourself a higher probability of success.

A good way of illustrating this is the following diagram:

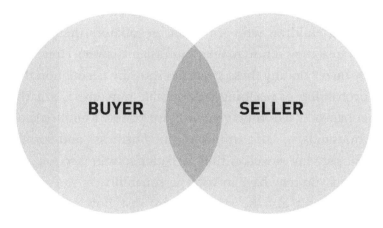

The only way you will ever reach an agreement is if all parties involved are negotiating in the shaded area. Now the inexperienced negotiator will assume that if the seller wants £10 million for their property and you are only willing to pay £8.5 million that there is no way that you can reach an agreement. As you will discover the shaded area (or the zone of agreement) is often not fixed and if you are flexible and creative can be greatly expanded to both parties' benefit.

Personality

Many books on negotiation will give you techniques and strategies that are "guaranteed" to work in every situation. This is rubbish. No single technique can be guaranteed to work in a negotiation for one very simple reason: you will be negotiating with *people*. This holds true whether you are negotiating with a trust, a family office or a company. Individuals will be involved. Human beings have complex emotions and their emotional states can vary on an hourly or daily basis. Therefore you are likely to need an array of techniques and strategies to conclude any negotiation successfully, even when dealing with one person.

You may already have noticed from your own experiences that personality has a large part to play in the negotiation process. Just think how many times you have put forward a rational and reasonable proposal or argument only to have it rejected outright, simply because the other party doesn't want to agree. The fact is that negotiations are often not entirely rational, which is why there is far more to it than simple logical reasoning. Even the most intelligent person can be a very bad negotiator if he or she forgets about or fails to acknowledge the emotional side of the process and the personalities of the individuals involved.

Unfortunately some people therefore assume that the best way to negotiate is to be a brash bully, refuse to compromise, and forever issue ultimatums. As you will learn, these people succeed in certain situations, but there is a far more subtle and successful way to negotiate, which will allow you to succeed far more often than the bully who does not compromise and walks away from what could have been a good deal just because his or her ego is too big to look at alternative solutions.

The first rule in a negotiation then is to always be nice but always be sceptical. People tend to prefer to do business with or sell their property to people they like. Ultimately you will also be trying to sell your proposition to them. Therefore they need to trust and respect you. They do not have to be your friend, but they do need to like you if you want to have a superior chance of achieving the best terms possible. In a very common situation, people with an emotional attachment to their home will only sell it to a family who they think will look after it in the same fashion.

However, you must always remain sceptical even if you like the people with whom you are negotiating. It is very rare for people to be entirely truthful. They may omit vital pieces of information and in some cases be genuinely dishonest. Indeed, they will very often not be entirely truthful because most people do not really know what they want from the negotiation. I will discuss this fact in more detail later. Suffice to say here that most people assume that the price is the most important factor, but there are often other factors that can be of equal or more importance.

Therefore it is vital that you do not have concrete presumptions about the other party's wishes. Throughout the negotiations you will need to ask lots of open-ended questions – both direct and indirect – to discover what they really want. You will have to listen intently to what people say and how they say it to see if it tallies with their previous statements and what they say they want (and what you think they want). Therefore if you are told by the seller or estate agent when you first meet them that they will only accept the asking price, ignore it.

People are motivated by self-esteem, prestige, recognition, and personal satisfaction more often than they are by money. Some peoples' egos make them believe that getting the highest price is the way to win. You may need to find other ways of satisfying their ego and letting them think they have won. If someone likes you or respects you they are likely to be more relaxed and honest. Therefore they will give you more information, which will allow you to conclude a successful negotiation. This is where the bullying negotiator misses huge opportunities, because he believes that price is all that matters and ultimatums are the best tactic to use. However, the more information you have, the easier it is to conclude a successful negotiation or resolve a dispute. Information about the sellers is often just as, if not more, important than the information about the property:

Questions you will need to answer

- What are the owner's motivations for selling?
- What information are they not giving you and why?
- What apart from money would make your offer attractive to them?
- How quickly do they need to move?
- What are their interests/hobbies?

These are just a small number of the questions you need to ask. A simple rule of thumb that you need to remember is that whoever has the best information in the negotiation is most likely to agree the best terms. The most useful information is often about the sellers rather than just their property, because as we have discussed, other factors can be much more important than price. Other questions you need to ask are:

- How long have you owned the property?
- Why do you want to sell it now?
- How did you settle on the asking price? Can you send me the comparables?
- Where are you moving to?
- How long has the apartment been on the market?
- How many viewings have there been?
- Do the sellers live at the property?
- How attached are they?
- What are their emotions? Is the property owned by an individual or a trust? (If the latter, they are likely to be more pragmatic.)
- What offers have you had?
- How quickly do you want to move?

The answers to these questions will inevitably lead to other questions:

You: "How long has the property been on the market and how many offers have you had?"

The Owner: "The property has been on for eight weeks and we haven't had any offers."

You: "Why do you think you haven't had any offers?"

Nobody wants to think that they are getting a poor deal. Everybody likes to think that they have "won" the negotiation. Nobody likes being told that they are wrong and nobody enjoys being interrogated. Therefore you have to be very careful about how one phrases questions and makes statements. The best way to approach the negotiation is to view it as finding a solution that helps the owners achieve their objectives while fulfilling all yours at the same time. This is something that you must keep at the forefront of your mind throughout the negotiations when dealing with not only the seller but also the estate agent. Rather counter-intuitively, what you *feel* during the negotiation is irrelevant. However, it is essential that the opposition remain happy, relaxed, and that they feel they are in control even though it will be you who is in control. Then you will be more likely to achieve a favourable outcome than you would if the sellers feel manipulated or backed into a corner. The following sections will show you how to do this.

Before we move on, it's important to mention the role of the estate agent, who is the person you will probably be interacting with despite the fact that he does not own the property. It is imperative that you build a good relationship with the agent from the moment you contact them about acquiring a home. Despite the fact that he is employed by the seller and legally obliged to achieve the best terms possible for the seller, the simple fact is that he is human. If he likes you, but his clients treat him with disdain (which often happens), then human nature dictates that he is likely to be more helpful to you. This is a simple but often overlooked point.

More importantly you must remember that his real motivation is not to find you your ideal home or sell his client's property on the best terms possible. His real motivation is the commission he will earn from the transaction. Therefore, he will probably baulk at offers and suggestions you make that he thinks will scupper the deal, so he will try to make you offer a higher price before going to the seller. Conversely, he will try to persuade the seller to see the merits of your proposal and to temper their requests so that the deal happens. It is essential that you remeber this dynamic.

It is also instructive to look at the figures. An estate agency will typically charge commission of two percent of the sale price of the property. If you're trying to acquire an apartment for £5 million and the difference in price between you and the seller is £250,000, this is fairly insignificant to the individual estate agent's commission. The total fee to the agency is £100,000 on £5 million, of which the individual agent may receive £25,000, but the £250,000 difference is only worth £1,250. He or she will not want this amount to be a deal breaker, and you can use this to your advantage.

The agents also have sales' targets, which mean the weaker agents will often lay their cards on the table when close to their sales' deadlines. Therefore it is wise to find out what targets they have and when. Always be motivational and enthusiastic about what they will get out of the deal and how easy you will make the transaction. Also make them feel that they have negotiated a good deal for their clients, e.g. "You are a great negotiator. I wouldn't normally increase my offer but on this one occasion I will."

By massaging the sellers' and estate agents' egos, you are far more likely to achieve a better result than you will by making them feel inferior.

Preparation

Why am I boring you with a section on preparation rather than showing you the proven techniques and strategies that we use? Quite simply because the best negotiators are also the most prepared. The simple truth is that most people enter negotiations having done no or minimal preparation, in the hope that they will be able to "wing it." This is partly because most people do not think that it is important to plan ahead and also partly because people assume that because they do not know what the other side's response will be that they will have to think on their feet and be spontaneous. This approach is likely to be fatal to your chances of negotiating a favourable outcome.

At the most basic level you need to have an objective. What are you trying to achieve in the negotiation? The answer needs to be very specific. Simply saying "I want to acquire the house on the best terms possible" is useless. What will you be willing to pay? What other terms are important? The problem with property transactions as I have already stated is that too many people focus solely on the price. We will come back to this point, but while we're going through price issues keep asking yourself the question: "What else could be included in the offer that would make it more attractive to the seller, but does not materially affect me?"

Price is obviously important. However, because no two properties are the same, property valuation is part science and part art. They will vary in size, volume, condition, views, lease length, and configuration. We also all have different tastes. Therefore, what represents fair value will to some degree be a subjective decision. It is essential, therefore, that you have a clear idea of what the property is worth to you as well as what the fair market value is. For example, if you are an artist, a house with a studio room with north facing light will be of greater value than it would be to someone who likes lots of direct sunlight.

Consequently, you will need to gather as much comparable data as possible. If you have carried out the research as suggested in previous chapters you should have found examples of similar properties that have sold for less than the one you wish to acquire. These may be slightly inferior but the seller may not know this and you can use them to justify your lower offer. Conversely you should also know about properties that have sold for more – were they better for some reason or did a buyer simply overpay? The more information you have the better you will be able to understand how they reached their valuation and anticipate their arguments and reactions.

Of course valuing the property is only one part of the process. You need to know much more information, including how long this house has been on the market, how many offers, how the market is behaving overall, and whether it is a buyers or sellers' market. If there have been multiple offers in a short space of time, then at what price? What position were the buyers in? If there have been no offers, why is that? Your strategy will vary depending on the answers.

While you are asking these questions, you will also be asking questions about the vendors to find out what their real motivations are. Most people sell property for a reason; perhaps they need a bigger house, are going through a divorce, the property is surplus to requirement, or they need funds quickly for a business deal. The price of the property is an important but coincidental factor. This is why you need to find out more about them. For example, someone may seem intransigent on price initially because they have not found a suitable residence to buy. However, once they have found a new home, they may become more flexible on price if you can guarantee a swift transaction. In fact, the purchase of their new home may be contingent upon a quick sale of their current one.

By asking questions about topics other than price, you will also gradually make the sellers consciously aware that there are other factors that they need to consider, which are important to the overall negotiation. This will create further flexibility and allow you to negotiate over a number of subjects. Questions to ask are:

- What is the condition of the roof, external areas and communal areas?
- Is the building well managed?
- What schedule of works is planned and what will be the cost?
- What hassle will be involved if the building is poorly managed (is this the reason for the sale)?
- What does the agent say is included in the sale?
- What would *you* like included in the sale? This could include items such as rugs, artwork, chandeliers, furniture, appliances, or parking spaces.
- What are the timescales for exchange and completion?
- Would they like to lease the property back for six months or a year?

Because the agents and sellers are so focussed on price you may find that your request for this information is met with these responses:

"We can discuss these points once we have agreed a

price," or "What is included will depend on the offer."

To which you simply respond with, "How can I make an offer or decide a price when I don't know on which items I am offering? Please ask the seller what he would be willing to include in the sale."

Even if they refuse to tell you, you should make a list of all the items which can be included in a negotiation, even if you don't want them. The more items and issues you can discuss and then ultimately concede without making your position weaker, the better. For example, you might initially ask for a piece of furniture to be included in the sale that you know the seller will not sell because it was a present with emotional value. You do not really care about it but you can make a fuss and make it seem like a big concession, which means that they may feel the need to reciprocate the concession with something that has some value for you.

You should grade all the items on this list in order of importance. You can then concede the less important points early on, but make them seem like big concessions. Then you can move to the important points and say, "I have been flexible on x, y and z. In the interest of fairness you can be flexible on this."

One note of caution. It is worth testing the other side after you have made two or three minor concessions to see if they will respond to the suggestion of them making a concession on the grounds of fairness. If they immediately refuse and say that those points have been agreed and are irrelevant to the negotiation, you need to change tactics. Whenever they make a demand you have to say to them, "Well, if you want to delay completion by three months, then what can you do to help me?" This immediately makes them realise that you are not going to bow to every point.

When you have finished your preparation you should have the following:

- Your walk away terms. This is the maximum you are willing to pay, the timeframe you are willing to offer, and a list of the minimum number of items that must be included. This will be your objective or bottom line. If you cannot achieve this then you will have to walk away from the house and continue the search.
- A list of comparable data to justify your valuation.
- A list of comparable data that the sellers/agents might use to justify their valuation.
- A list of items that can be included in the negotiations. These should be graded in order of importance to you.
- A list of the questions you have asked and the respective answers (about the property, the market and the vendors themselves).
- A list of the questions to which you have not received a response (or a satisfactory response) but which you need answering.
- A list of questions that the seller might have for you and the respective answers. Putting yourself in the vendors' shoes will give you a better perspective of what they will want.

You should have these to hand whenever you speak

to the other party so that you have all the information you require. Then before every meeting, telephone call or email you should also consider the following:

- What is the topic you want to cover? What do you want to achieve and what is the objective of the meeting?
- What questions must you ask? What answers are likely and what further questions?
- What information will you need to hand?
- How will you convey your message?
- What will you say if you reach an impasse?
- What concessions can you make? Put these in order
- How will they react? What questions will they have? Prepare good answers and have the relevant information to hand.
- How big is their ego? What are their motivations?
- What is the strategy? What tactics will you employ?

This may seem like overkill, but if you are focussed and prepared you are more likely to achieve your objective. The most successful negotiators are those who take small progressive steps to hit a lot of seemingly small objectives. However, once you add all of these up the compounded effect will be huge. Each tiny objective and telephone call can prove pivotal to the overall negotiation. Therefore you must be prepared for each contact and if you have done the above then you will be in a much stronger position than 99.9% of the people with whom you will negotiate.

So how do we use this?

9. Strategies

Here are the basic strategies that you should know and use when negotiating.

1. Always be a reluctant buyer

Remember the negotiation starts *before* you put forward an offer. It really starts the second you speak to the agent, when you must immediately position yourself as the perfect buyer. Consequently you must be very careful about the information you give away. This is especially true when looking around the property. Effusing about the property will make it much harder to buy it at the best price because you will have shown your hand (although this can be rectified as you will see in good cop/bad cop later). If you really like it, show interest, but also point out the negatives by saying, for example, "It's nice but I don't like the way the bedrooms are configured. I also think the price is too high. I would probably consider it at the right price. What do they realistically want for it?"

Remember the agent really just wants the deal so he may tell you the actual figure as far as he knows. Consequently you may be able to achieve even less than the figure he gives you.

If you don't like the property, be polite and explain to the agent the issues so that he or she does not show you inadequate properties in the future. However, do not go into too much detail. You want to show that you are a serious buyer who can move quickly when you see the right property. You also want the agent to like and respect you, so that you're the first person he calls when a new property is available.

When viewing a property you might also say to the agent, "The asking price seems a little bold. What price did you value it at?" Quite often they will admit that they valued it for less; or if they say that this is their price, ask them what comparables they used for their valuation. Take notes and ask them to send you the details. It is also advisable to speak to other agents about the property to get their opinion. If they give you an opinion, ask them what they have sold recently that matches the property and ask them to email you the details. If you ask enough agents you may discover that one or two of them had valued the property when the seller was trying to decide which agency to use. They may give you their valuations and even the view that the incumbent agency overvalued it. All of this is fantastic information that you can use later in the negotiation.

Flinch at the stated price, both physically and verbally. Remember the negotiation is already underway when you visit a property. So if you're looking around a property and you like it, casually ask the agent, "What's the asking price for this?" even if you know the answer. When he responds, simply say "What?" in an agitated manner and flinch or raise your eyebrows. Then say nothing and just look at him. Very often the agent will start trying to justify the price, and even tell you that you can buy it for less and give you a figure. (Remember this is before you have even done any in depth research). Either way you will gain valuable information. The flinch is a tactic that can be used whenever a demand is made or price discussed. It can also be used successively on the same point. A weak negotiator will just keep lowering the price.

Above all you must know your walk away terms – sorry to repeat this, but it's vital. This is your objective. You must not waver from it unless compelling evidence becomes apparent that shows that your calculations are wrong. However, it's essential to realise that you will not always be able to negotiate a good deal or even a fair deal. This is why you must have a walk away price. It is the maximum you will be willing to pay or the minimum terms you would be willing to accept. If you stick to your walk away limit, you cannot lose the negotiation or make an expensive mistake.

Needless to say, once you set your walk away limit, you must never let your emotions take over. There will always be another property on the market.

Always ask for more than you can get or want. Never put forward your best offer, as this leaves no room for you to negotiate. Therefore you must offer a lower price than you would pay, ask for numerous superfluous items to be included such as artwork, cars, and other items that you would be happy to concede at a later date. You also need to ask for either quicker or slower timescales than you require, a lower deposit for exchange, and alternative payment terms. The more items the better as it widens the scope of the negotiation and deflects from the price.

This does not mean that you should ever make a pointlessly low offer that is based on no research. However, you can stretch your research to give you a plausible reason for your offer. You should never feel embarrassed to put forward a low offer or include lots of additional items. If you do feel embarrassed, psychologically this means you are starting from a weak position, which is no good. So have confidence in your research. When you know that your offer is within reason you won't feel nervous or concerned that the other side will feel insulted or not take you seriously. And you will also have seen from your research that many properties are massively overvalued. Are the owners and agents embarrassed? Certainly not, so nor should you be.

There are other practical reasons for asking for more than you think you will get or even want:

- People never believe your first offer is your best. They expect to negotiate.
- A property negotiation in Prime Central London often differs from a business negotiation in one key fact: you may not directly speak to the owner, and instead will be dealing with the estate agent. You may not even know who the sellers are. Therefore it is much harder to find information on the other side. You need to test the boundaries, as your assumptions about what they may

be willing to accept may be completely wrong, just as can the agent's assumptions.

- It will help realign the seller's expectations. For example, if the property is on the market for £5 million and you know it is worth £4.25 million, you may decide to offer £3.3 million. Of course you need to do this in a non-confrontational manner as you do not want an argument. Remember the sellers' ego is more important than yours, so you might say, "I know that you're asking £5 million for your apartment based on the facts that you have and that you think that that is fair. I may have overlooked something but based on the research we have done it seems that £3.3 million is the level we should be discussing, so £3.3 million is our offer."

The seller will realise that you have done your research and that you are simply opening the negotiations. You now have a framework within which to negotiate, i.e. £3.3 million to £5 million. If your walk away price is £4.25 million you have also positioned yourself so that if you have to agree at that level the seller can feel that he has "won" because in contrast to your £950,000 increase he has only come down £750,000 from his initial position.

Even if for some reason you have offered the asking price, the seller will invariably think you can offer more. In the worst cases the seller may think that the estate agent has undervalued the property and will just increase the price by a large margin, even if the price you were willing to pay was a premium. Alternatively, if the property is new to the market, they will thank you for your offer but not accept it, saying they want to let other people view the house before they decide. Of course, in some cases they might accept your first offer right off. Personally this would annoy me, because it means that we could have negotiated a lower price. It would also concern me that they had accepted my first offer so easily; I would assume that there was an issue with the property and they were happy to unload it.

2. Ignore high asking prices and high offers

I have often seen properties that remain on the market for months because of owners who have turned down a high price early in the marketing and have then refused further sensible offers because they cannot bring themselves to accept a lower price. This highlights a number of points:

- Most sellers do not really understand how to reach a walk away price. They are using their gut or arbitrary figures.
- An offer means nothing until the deal has been concluded. There is a huge difference between having an offer of £5 million and actually selling the house for that amount – something that many sellers forget.
- Agents often overvalue properties to win the instruction. They can sometimes be embarrassed to admit this later, especially when their client has turned down a good offer thinking the agents' valuation was correct. You can sometimes use such situations to your advan-

tage. Firstly find out when the offer was and at what level. Is that buyer still in the picture or have they bought? What you must remember is that most people are poor negotiators. In this case the seller may have turned down a good early offer because they were greedy, lacked motivation, were underprepared, or didn't know the fair value of their house. However, you know what fair value is and what your walk away price is. You can offer significantly lower than the initial offer; for example, £4 million is the asking price and an initial offer of £3.6 million has been rejected. The fair value is £3.5 million, so you can offer £2.9 million. This has a big psychological impact. Even if they still want £3.6 million you will have moved them away from £4 million and they realise that £3.6 million may even be a stretch. Now they should consider themselves lucky to get even £3.5 million.

Buyers are often put off by overpriced properties and refuse to negotiate. They shouldn't be. It probably means that you will be negotiating in a vacuum, and as long as you know your ceiling price then you cannot lose.

Conversely, you don't want to try to be too clever. Sometimes the asking price could be a bargain, so it may make sense to pay up and get the property off the market. If you try to be too clever somebody else may spot that the price is too low and snap it up from under your nose. However, a word of caution: you do not want the vendors to realise that you are getting a bargain, so you need to plan your approach carefully.

- Good cop/bad cop. One half of the buying team can indicate that they love the property, while the other voices their concerns. The reason this technique works so well is that it appears honest, guileless and open. The good cop is there to ensure that the agent thinks you are worth his persuasion while the bad cop plays the reluctant buyer. This will encourage the agent to let slip vital information to try to get you to bid if it seems that your interest is waning - for example, "To be honest we didn't value it at this and the seller is now quite motivated as they have found somewhere to buy, so it's worth making an offer." This is when you ask, "What did you value it at?" and "What do you think they will accept?" You may then decide to use the flinch after the answer to this question!

- "You have to do better than that." This is similar to the flinch and can be used at any time in a negotiation. You can use it on salespeople when they are giving you a price for a product or service. They will quite often give you an immediate reduction, to which you say again, "You'll have to do better than that!" This sentence alone can save you thousands of pounds a year. However, when acquiring a property the agent may use this tactic on *you*, and you may be tempted to increase your offer. You should not do this, and instead respond by saying, "I've offered a very fair price and terms. Why do I have to do better?" Or simply say, "Give me a number." The agent needs to justify his position, so use this to get more information from him. If the market is in your favour you may even want to go a step further by saying, "I have offered a very fair price and terms, why do I have to do better? No-one else has even bid and this is more than I had planned to offer. Instead of increasing my price why aren't you reducing yours?"

- Timing the offer. When should you make an offer and when do you increase it? This will very much depend on a number of factors. Again information is the key, so you need to know the following: What is the state of the market? How many interested parties are there? How motivated is the seller? How far apart are you in price? What deadlines do they have? What type of people are they? Do they make decisions quickly or slowly? How long has the property been on the market?

Sometimes it will be beneficial to offer immediately. Conversely it can pay to wait days or even weeks to make an offer. A simple rule of thumb, though, is not to look overly keen. Keep up the image of the reluctant buyer unless there are obvious advantages to moving swiftly – for example, if the sellers need to move quickly and you can prove that you can move fast too. When sellers are under genuine time pressure then you will be able to achieve a lower price in exchange for speed.

- Evidence. Anyone can say they can move quickly, but it is much more powerful when you can prove the point. If you have done your preparation as described in the very first chapter of this book, you should be able to provide documentation to back your case:

proof of funds, letters from solicitors, accountants, etc. A motivated seller is more likely to accept your offer if you have these items.

It is for this reason that offers should almost always be made in writing. It's a simple fact that people take written offers and information more seriously than when delivered verbally. Personally, I send offers in an attachment to my emails, as this means that the agent can easily forward it to their client, who may not always live in London. If the negotiation is going to be protracted I might make a couple of early offers verbally if I know they will be rejected. I then follow these up with a written offer, as this indicates that we are getting to the "business end" of the negotiation and that the early jousting has stopped. The agent and seller will then believe that we are getting nearer to our maximum offer, even if this isn't necessarily the case. Obviously you will need to vary this tactic depending on the situation.

The strategies and tactics outlined above are predominantly for the start of the negotiation – to establish price flexibility before you have even made an offer and what is required in the initial offer. Now if you implement these ideas you'll be aware that your opening offer is likely to be rejected, which is when one implements the "middle game" strategies:

- Questions. You must keep asking open-ended questions to discover more information about the other party. You will also need to repeat questions (although phrase them differently) to check that the original answers were accurate and still valid. Questions you should ask:

- What did the vendor say about the offer?
- What figure did he say he would trade at?
- What price do you think he would sell for?
- How serious are they about selling?
- What two things could we offer other than money that would make our offer more attractive to them?

Then collate all the information and work out the next bid. Whatever you do, do *not* immediately increase your offer. If you do you will at best show that you have a lot more money to offer and at worst you will seem desperate. So take at least a few hours or a few days before you increase your offer.

- Taper your offers. The amounts that you increase your offers by must not be random. They must be carefully considered, as the increases in the offer will elicit different reactions and assumptions. For example, let's say you have initially bid £7 million on a property that you feel is worth £9 million and the asking price is £11 million. If you then raise your bid all the way to £8.75 million, the seller will assume that you will be willing to pay £9.5 million or more. Quite simply you have conceded too much ground too quickly, which is a similar mistake to making your initial offer your best offer (this is assuming that they have simply rejected your offer and you have received no further information). In general, you want to increase your offer or reduce the number of items you wish to be included on an incremental basis that decreases with each new offer. Your incremental increase need not be in the cash price; you can "increase" your offer by taking away features that you wanted ("OK, we'll accept one parking place rather than two").

In this example you might go from £7 million to £7.75 million, then to £8.3 million, then to £8.7 million, etc. The smaller increases will indicate that you are getting closer to your maximum price. You should taper your concessions so that it appears that you have reached your maximum price before you actually have.

Of course, you should try not increase your price unless there has been a concession on the other side. Whenever an offer is rejected you must ask for a counter-offer and gain more information before you make any further offers.

Hopefully they will accept the offer that is below your walk away price. But if not, you can increase your final offer by a larger amount by using the "white knight" strategy, which we will discuss later.

- The speed at which you make these increases will also have an effect. Sometimes it is advisable not to increase your offer for weeks or even months if the sellers are not willing to negotiate; quite often this means that they are not serious sellers, so you do not need to waste your time or miss out on other properties by focussing all your attention on this one property.
- You should not allow yourself to be intimidated by the seller. It is quite possible that when you put forward

your low bid that the seller will say, "£7.75 million is a ridiculous offer. We are asking £12m. Either make a sensible offer or stop wasting my time." Now an inexperienced negotiator might then offer £9.5 million or even his £10 million walk away price, expecting the seller to acknowledge that this is a fair price and to agree. However, this negotiator has immediately made a massive concession and is now negotiating in a range of £10 million to £12 million. The seller will again believe that he can convince you to pay an extra £250,000 to £500,000, if not more, and you have no room for negotiation. Therefore the negotiations are likely to end in deadlock or you will overpay.

A better negotiator will realise that in this situation the seller has done nothing to defend his price. He has effectively used "the flinch" to get you to increase your offer. You need to respond by providing some of the comparables you have found to justify your price and say, "My research shows that £7.75 million is the level at which we should be negotiating, but maybe I have missed something. How have you reached a price of £12 million?"

Once, a client asked me to not put forward the low offer I had suggested, on the grounds that the seller might refuse to deal with us. If you're having similar thoughts, don't worry about this. In over sixteen years of acquiring property I have never had a situation where the seller refused to sell to us because of the low initial offer. That's not to say that we acquire every property we offer on;

sometimes you have to walk away if the other side is intractable. But if you employ these steps and strategies you'll have a higher probability of success.

One of the reasons that we are not scared of advising clients to walk away from a property, and why we carefully calculate the walk away price, is that there will always be other properties available. You will be speaking to the agent about other properties on a weekly basis anyway, so he will keep you informed of any movement on the property on which you had offered. In fact he will probably be trying to get you to increase your offer so that he can earn his commission, in which case simply say to him, "We're still interested, but we need the owners to show that they're serious about selling, so please tell them that we need a counter-offer."

Quite often we are able to show our clients two or three properties that are suitable. If this happens to you there is always likely to be one property that stands out for you, but it's important to remain as unemotional as possible. If the other properties are also good you should not discount them entirely because the more options you have the better you will handle the negotiations as you will not be desperate to buy that one property. Consequently, in case an equally good or better opportunity arises you should keep looking for properties while the negotiations are underway.

It should also be noted that you are entirely within your rights to offer on multiple properties simultaneously. In fact when we do this I ensure that all the agents and sellers know that we're bidding on other properties, because it puts us in a strong position. There is nothing unethical about doing this. After all, the sellers are happy to have multiple buyers bid on their property. The key to success when making multiple bids is to work out your walk away price and terms for each of the properties. As you will probably be able to grade the properties in order of preference you will have a sliding scale of what will be acceptable for each property, and you can negotiate on each accordingly using all the principles we have covered here.

In such situations you may want to say something like, "We've found three houses that we like, so really it is now just about price. We have decided that the fairest thing to do is to ask all three owners to give us their lowest prices, so that we can proceed quickly rather than put everyone through a convoluted process."

- Splitting the difference. This may seem like the simple solution to any impasse you might have in the negotiation. For, example, you may want to pay £4 million, while the seller wants £4.5 million; and the seller then suggests agreeing at £4.25 million because it is the middle point. However:

  Four million pounds may be the fair price according to your research, so you will not be getting a good deal. Therefore you should respond by saying, "I've carried out a lot of research on this. All the comparable properties that have sold recently show that your apartment is worth £3.9 million. However, because I like it and I have spent time on this, I am willing to offer £4 million. Ultimately I should be trying to acquire this for £3.8 million, but I will stick to my £4 million if you agree today."

You should also never be the person to recommend splitting the difference. Firstly, because you want the seller to make the suggestion so that he thinks that you have agreed and he has "won." Secondly, it shows you that their negotiation range has changed. For example, let's say you have offered £3 million. They are at £3.5 million and you would be happy to transact at £3.25 million. If they offer to split the difference you are already in a good position. However, instead of immediately accepting the offer you say, "So you will sell your apartment for £3.25 million [and list all the other points you have agreed], is that correct?" They will confirm but you do not accept. You continue to negotiate but the range is now £3 million-£3.25 million. Umm and ahh, saying that you just cannot reach that price, the apartment is not worth it, etc. If they're tough they'll say, "Take it or leave it." But quite often they will offer to split the difference *again*, to £3.125 million. You can repeat this until it fails to work or you can simply accept the improved terms. The key is that you're accepting *their* proposal, so psychologically they will be more tied in to the agreement.

- Time pressure. Numerous studies have proven that people tend to wait until the last moment to reach an agreement, but that they are then willing to accept sub-optimal terms. Because of this, it is vital that you do not reveal that you have a timeline unless you can use this to create a deadline for the other side. For example, you may try to speed up the process by saying, "We need to buy a house in the next month. If we do not, we'll rent a property for a year and take our time." Remember to keep testing for time pressure throughout the negotiation, as people's circumstances can change.

Conversely, you must test deadlines. If someone tries to impose deadlines on you, you must check how serious they are. If you are told, for example, that you have to make a decision in twenty-four hours, simply say that you will be away on business for two days and will be in meetings the entire time, and ask if it can't wait until you return so that you can give it the attention it deserves. It's important to note that this approach is not antagonistic or confrontational. You have not said "no" and made them "lose" this mini-negotiation. It is a considered response that cannot bruise their ego. However, their reaction to your response will tell you whether the deadline is serious or not.

If you need to move swiftly, but you know the other side needs to move swiftly too, you may decide to slow the negotiations to panic them. Conversely if you need to move quickly but the other side is dithering, you can create time pressure for them by saying, for example, "If you do not accept the offer by the end of today then I am sorry but we will have to bid on another property, as this is taking so long." This is a risky ploy but you may have to use it.

- Time and energy. The more invested people are in a negotiation then the more likely they are to want to agree a deal. This means you should try to get the other side to invest as much time and energy as possible, for example by asking them to produce management accounts, planning information or building regulations before you offer. You must also be aware that the agent may try to do the same to you. If a property is over budget, they may suggest you put in an offer under the pretence that the seller might accept a low offer. However, this may just be a ploy to get you emotionally attached to the property so that you stretch your budget. The same applies with a property on which you seem to have negotiated good terms. The seller may try to raise the price at the last minute, thinking that you are unlikely to walk away due to the investment you have put into the purchase. Another possible scenario is that the survey may highlight serious issues but the vendor is nonetheless unwilling to compromise on price. Again you may feel tempted to agree to the purchase because of the time and effort you have put into the negotiation and the costs (surveys, solicitors) that have been incurred. Therefore, you must be very aware of how invested you are and try to ensure that the other party's investment exceeds yours.

- Ultimatums. I try to avoid these, as they are confrontational and also make it hard for the other side to win. I certainly rarely use the "take it or leave it" bluster unless I am sure that the other side will concede and that it will not jeopardise the agreement. However, sometimes you do need to give the other side a strong nudge. A more effective way of handling the situation would be to say, "Unfortunately this is the maximum I can offer you for the house. You just need to decide whether it works for you or not." It almost sounds like an apology but the message is clear: We can't offer any more. The fact that it is apologetic in tone makes them almost feel sorry for you and can elicit some sympathy. This makes the other side feel strong and in control, and gives the illusion that they have won by extracting your every last penny, even if you could pay more.

Always try to leave the option to return to the negotiation e.g. "I can't buy the house for £6 million but do come back to me if your client changes their mind." This is much better than saying, "£5.5 million is my final offer – take it or leave it," as it does not make the other side feel as though they are losing face by coming back to the table. Instead they can feel that they have made a rational decision to reach an agreement rather than bending to the might of your will. If it was you, which do you think is likely to be the more successful approach?

Of course the sellers may use this tactic on you by saying, for example, "I am sorry we can't accept a penny less; otherwise we will not be able to buy our next home." In this instance it often pays to stick to your price but to position it so that the other side has won. Instead of conceding you would say that you are very sorry and that you cannot go any higher, and thank them for their time. Then wait for a length of time to pass (you will need to judge this by the speed of the negotiation to date and what is happening in the market). You can then go back and make a small concession such as, for example, "I'm sorry. We have checked our finances and £6 million is our absolute maximum. We would, however, be willing to extend the completion date and lend you our villa in Tuscany as a token of gratitude." This may not always work but it will improve your chances as they will feel that they have won.

- The white knight. When playing this ultimatum game, you may be concerned about how you can increase your offer if it has been rejected. The simple way to do this is by using the white knight gambit. After a certain time lapse you can call the agent or seller and say, "Have the owners had any further thoughts on our offer of £6 million?" If the agent says he doesn't know, ask him to speak to them and ask what the situation is. They may come back with a counter offer of £6.125 million, or they may restate £6.25 million. If it's the former you can either hold out for £6 million, try to negotiate a reduction from £6.125 million, or accept the counter offer. You do need to have a plausible excuse for suddenly finding the extra money, however. This is where the white knight comes to your rescue. You simply say that you have inherited the money, a relative has kindly offered to lend the money for a year, or the trustees have allowed you to sell some shares; whatever the most plausible reason may be. The key is that the other side must feel that you have folded to their counter-offer and not that you had the money there the whole time.

- Be creative. For example, if you see lots of pictures in the house of the owners on holiday, you may offer them two weeks at your villa or on your yacht. Send photographs of these to increase the power of the offer. If you learn that they collect stamps, figurines, cars, etc., is there anyone you know who could offer them a unique experience? For example, a car fanatic may like to race classic cars at Brooklands. It's a simple fact that people value things about which they are keenly interested much more highly than the actual cost. So even if you have to pay £20,000 to arrange a day's racing at Brooklands, the perceived value to the seller may be much higher and will result in a greater reduction. The key is to be creative and as ever to gain as much information as possible about the seller.

- Conspiracy theory. If you tell someone something in confidence, they are more likely to let slip information to you. It's human nature. However, you must remember that the agent works for the seller. More importantly, they want to get the deal done so that they can earn their commission. Therefore it can sometimes be useful to ask for their help. Call them and say, "You and I both want to do a deal but I just cannot pay the price they are saying they want. What do you think might improve my offer? Think outside the box on this." If the agent is on good terms with the seller they may have some vital information. Perhaps they're a collector of wine, and you may have a case of Petrus that may swing the deal.

3. How to avoid being pressurised

However prepared you may be, there will be times when you're caught off-guard by a question, and there may be occasions when the seller or the agent will try to put you under pressure. In these instances it can be easy to become confrontational by rejecting the demand, or to be rushed into giving an inaccurate or poorly thought-out answer. The simple way out is to defer to a higher authority. Even if there is no one you need to ask, say that you cannot give an answer until you have spoken to someone else:

"I'll need to check that my husband/wife is happy with that."

"I'll need to ask my financiers/solicitors/tax advisers whether that is possible. I'll let you know as soon as they have given me an answer."

- Telephone calls and emails. There is a compulsion in the modern day to answer phones and respond immediately to emails. In a negotiation it can be a truly expensive mistake because you're unlikely to be prepared, and will put the other side at an advantage. If you do answer the phone, initially listen to what they have to say without answering any questions. Then simply say that now is not a convenient time and you will call them back. You can then evaluate what you have been told or asked. It may be tempting to ask questions when you are called. However, I would be careful. It's possible that an unprepared question could give away your mindset or position.

- What happens if the seller asks you for your best and final offer? This is a ploy, whether the sellers realise it or not. Your fear is that you think this is your last chance to negotiate. It is not. The first thing to ask is how long exactly you have to decide. If the timeline is vague then it is likely not to be a serious demand. If you are told by noon the following day, say that you are busy over the next forty-eight hours, and ask if it can't wait until the end of the week. Again, if they waiver then it's not a serious deadline. If they are adamant that you do need to offer quickly, you must find out why. If there are no other bidders then they may be under time pressure themselves or are trying to flush out your highest offer. Depending on the situation you may choose to stick to your current offer or to increase it slightly. I would strongly advise you *not* to put forward your best offer. If your "best and final" offer is rejected, that is not the end of the negotiation. Simply phone the agent and say, "I'm sorry we couldn't do business on this occasion. We have all spent a lot of time on this. Out of interest, what figure would they have traded at?" If they give you a figure then you can decide on the next step in the negotiation. If they do not know, ask them to ask the vendor, strictly out of interest.

Of course, you will sometimes be asked to put forward your best and final bid or enter into a sealed bid, when there really are other bidders, as this is a quick way of bringing the matter to a close. Depending on how you approach business there are two ways of approaching this:

Firstly, simply put forward the highest offer you are willing to put forward, i.e. your walk away price and terms. If you win the sealed bid then that's fantastic. If not, you still haven't "lost." Another party has simply decided to overpay for a property and you simply continue looking for another opportunity. The biggest mistake people make in sealed bid situations is to try to be too clever. I'm often asked what percentage above the last offer they should bid or how far below their walk away price they should try to pitch the offer. You don't know what the other bidders will do. You can only control your side. Obviously you should make enquiries about the other bidders; if you're a cash buyer and they require a mortgage and already seem stretched then you may not go all the way to your walk away price. However, if you are happy with your walk-away price, which you should be, then there is nothing wrong with offering this.

Secondly, you may try an offer that is not your maximum with the view to increasing it if you do not win the sealed bid. This tactic can work, but is not regarded as very ethical. If the seller is ethical, then he or she may decide to ignore your increased offer. You will hear that you have been unsuccessful after the winning bidder has been contacted and a verbal agreement has been made. Indeed for them to renege on the agreement you may have to offer considerably more than the winning bidder. It is possible, therefore, that you will have to pay more than you would if your walk away price had been the highest offer.

Please note that you cannot put forward an offer saying that you will bid two percent more than the highest bidder. The agents will not accept these and will advise you as such when they inform you of a sealed bid situation.

Throughout this process you should emphasize the strength of your position, e.g. you can move quickly, be flexible on completion, will let them keep the chandeliers, etc. You should always include a letter from your solicitors and financiers.

4. Traits of a good negotiator

- Patience. This is an essential for negotiators. If you are under time pressure, this will cause you to be impatient and try to rush the negotiation. Again this will be hugely detrimental. The problem is that you'll be focussed on what you want, and you'll not be seeking enough information from the other side and you will not be paying attention to the information you are receiving. Therefore vital snippets of info or subtle changes in the other side's conversational manner will be missed. In the worst instances you will appear desperate, which is when you'll lose any power in the negotiation. This is why taking notes, being prepared for each meeting and telephone call, and setting agendas are so useful. They force you to slow down, be calm, and listen. This will convey to the other side that they are dealing with someone in total control. That is not to say you can never be loud or aggressive or impatient, but if you are it will be because you have *planned* to be and not because you have lost control.

- Emotional detachment. The key to being patient is to remain emotionally detached. If you become emotionally attached to a property (or whatever the subject of the negotiation may be) you will be in a much weaker position. You're likely to become impatient because you will be focussing too much on what you want rather than understanding and keeping the seller's perspective in focus. This is likely to make you confrontational, which will in turn make the sellers confrontational, and then rational behaviour bows to egotistical demands.

Of course, the seller may well become agitated without reason. This is because they're either not skilled negotiators, or they are skilled and are using it as a ploy. Therefore if you have a situation where the seller is becoming emotional it is useful to keep asking questions, as they may let something slip. However, if it is creating a deadlock or their emotions are having a negative effect on the negotiation then it will be sensible to deflect from the point causing the issue. If they're becoming angry about the price, for example, simply move the negotiation forward by saying, "If we can agree on price, what are the best completion dates for you? Will you accept a five percent deposit on exchange? What is included in the sale?" And then negotiate these points. Once this is done you can return to the original issue: "Great, we have agreed on all the outstanding points. Now let's agree on price." Quite often the initial aggression will have gone and you will be able to work together to reach an agreement. However, sometimes it may be necessary to halt the negotiations for a day or two to allow the other side to cool down.

- Gazumping. This is the term used to describe a situation where you have reached an agreement with the seller, who then later says he wants more money because they've been offered more by another party, or he simply feels that you should be paying more. In such instances you are likely to become understandably angry because the seller appears to have behaved in an unfair or unethical fashion. Try to keep your emotions under control, however, and look at the bigger picture.

  If you have tested to see whether this is just an empty ploy and found that not to be the case, you need to decide whether the new terms still work for you. This is where you need to remain emotionally detached. Even though it may not be as good a deal as you had initially agreed on, it may still be a good acquisition so you should then proceed. Try not to let your ego get in the way and refuse to proceed, as this is effectively cutting your nose off to spite your face. If the property is your ideal home that you will love for the next ten or twenty years, the few hours or days of irritation will be worth the trade. However, you must demand something in exchange, such as, "If we agree to pay the increased price what will you do for us?" Or, "If we pay this we want x, y and z included, and to exchange today." (Assuming your solicitor is happy that everything is in order.)

- Organisation. Because there are numerous ways to reach an agreement, you'll need to try to assess all the possible options. It is essential that you have all the documentation, facts and figures to hand. You must take notes during every conversation or discussion with the seller and estate agent. You must keep times and dates of calls, emails, etc., and whom you spoke to as well as the actual details of the call or meeting itself.

It's particularly important to make a note of all the concessions made by you and the other party, so that you can be sure that there can be no confusion. If the negotiation is protracted then you should send a weekly update to the estate agent and seller confirming the points that have been agreed. This avoids confusion and makes it impossible for the other side to later say, "I never agreed to that…"

Throughout any negotiation always check the progress.

"Is this everything that you want? If we resolve these items do we have an agreement?" If the answer is "no," then you must ask, "What is still outstanding?" Remember if the negotiations are protracted then both your and the seller's situations may change and different things may become more or less important. It is essential to double check.

- Creativity / solution oriented. There may be situations where you like a house but cannot afford it even at a fair or even favourable price. Again you should explore other options: Will you have the additional funds in a year or two? Would the seller be prepared to accept 80% of the funds now and 10% in a year and the balance in two years?

- Non-confrontational. Always be polite and never get into an argument. It will create more problems even if you are right because of the personalities involved. However, this does not mean that you can allow yourself to be bullied. The key is to maintain your calm and be unemotional.

Never tell the other side that they are wrong even when they produce comparables that are clearly misleading. Again this is a psychological point. People do not like to be told that they are wrong. The way to approach this is to feign confusion. You need to say, "I'm sorry I may well have misunderstood something here. Please can you show me how comparable x (their data) is a better comparable for the value than a, b, c, or d?" This will have a much more powerful effect, as they will have to think about why they are expecting a high price when the evidence suggests otherwise. It will also create a collaborative atmosphere for the negotiation rather than an argumentative one. Which do you think is more likely to bring about a successful outcome? Indeed this approach is often very effective if you use it before you even put forward an offer.

If the seller continues to expect a high price, you may be dealing with someone who is not serious about selling or will only sell if someone pays an absurd premium. In this instance you should ask, "Why do you expect me to pay a significant premium for your property?" The answer is likely to reveal the seller's real motivations. Alternatively if the comparables you have used include properties that are on the market you might say, "So unless I'm mistaken, what you are really saying is that at the price you're asking I would be much better advised to acquire property b. Is that correct?" Sometimes you have to paint a very clear picture in the seller's head about the situation before they realise how extreme their position is.

5. Useful phrases and questions

If you put forward an offer and the agent says it is too low, simply respond, "What do you think is the right price?" Very often they will provide a lower price than the asking price. This is useful information.

If someone demands a delayed completion or a quick exchange always ask, "Why would you like to move this swiftly/slowly?" Even if the suggestion suits you, ask the question and make it seem like an issue. They may let slip vital information or make an unexpected concession.

If you reach a deadlock, asking hypothetical questions can help you find solutions:

"What if I paid cash?"

"What if I offered x but delayed completion for six months?"

"What if I paid x but included my Aston Martin?"

"What if I staggered the payments?"

The answers will help you gauge whether they are totally inflexible or if there are alternative solutions that can be pursued.

You can feign ignorance to attract help or get information: "I'm sorry, I must be not seeing something. How did they decide on this price?"

Proof this works...

"When we found our ideal property they advised us on the negotiation tactics and developed a strategy, which they then executed. Consequently we were not pressurised during the negotiations and thanks to Mercury's negotiation skills we bought the house at a much lower price than we would have achieved. In fact we bought it for less than our initial bid would have been!"

– Mr & Mrs Evans, Notting Hill

10. The Final Hurdle

Remember that agreeing the price is only the first phase. The agreement is not legally binding until contracts have been exchanged. Over fifteen percent of purchases fail between the completion of negotiations and the exchange of contracts. The legal process can be extremely drawn out and the longer it takes the more likely it is that the deal will collapse. The seller might receive a higher offer or think that he is selling for too little.

We always demand a period of exclusivity to avoid other buyers trying to increase their bids. This can be structured in various ways and should be discussed with your solicitor before you include it in your offer. However, we advise against putting down a non-refundable deposit, as the risk is often not worth it and we have never had to go down this route. (There are some situations where a non-refundable deposit may make sense. However, these situations are rare and will also be determined by your attitude to risk.)

Ultimately, it is your responsibility to make sure everything proceeds smoothly. You need to co-ordinate your financier, solicitor and surveyor. Remember your solicitor will probably not see the property, so you need to give him or her as much information as possible and flag any potential points of concern.

You also need to ensure that the other side is acting

swiftly. If they have a solicitor who does not specialise in property you need to ensure that the estate agent is on top of the situation.

There may be numerous third parties involved as well including managing agents, The Grosvenor Estate, English Heritage, the local council etc. You need to ensure that your team is ahead of the game and that the seller's side is providing the information in a timely fashion. If you do not, you must be prepared for the frustration of losing what could be your ideal home.

You will also need to liaise closely with your surveyor. If you have concerns about a crack on a structural wall, damp problems, etc., it is best to highlight these when you book the survey. Although the surveyor will invariably spot them, it will put your mind at ease if he addresses them directly in his report. In older buildings, thin cracks may be inconsequential and therefore may only receive a passing comment in the surveyor's report.

The type of survey you choose will depend on the style and age of the building. You need to have a member of the Royal Institute of Chartered Surveyors (RICS) complete the survey. However, you may also want to consider having a damp and timber survey, gas and electrical checks, and a drain survey carried out on the property. You must send copies of all surveys to your solicitor. If you're raising finance to purchase the property, do not rely on the lender's survey. Their survey is purely to ensure that the property will cover their liability if you fail to make your payments. It is not a structural survey.

One of the major reasons transactions fail is because buyers panic and overreact when the surveys or searches reveal problems. Much of London's housing stock was built before 1920, so it is almost inevitable that there will be some issues. There may also be issues with building regulations, the lease, etc. There are a number of solutions to these problems including renegotiating the terms and arranging indemnity insurance. In most cases the issues can be resolved if you have a good solicitor and surveyor representing you. Therefore you must explore every apparent defect before you decide not to buy the property. Many a good opportunity has been abandoned simply because an inexperienced buyer has taken fright at the last moment rather than undertaking the necessary research and making an objective decision on the problem in hand.

Remember that there are two different categories of defect. The first category includes the obvious defects that you know are repairable and on which you can place a monetary value. For example, if the oil-burning furnace in the basement dates from 1930 and is at the end of its service life, you can reasonably tell the seller that the price needs to come down by an appropriate sum to pay for a new system. The same goes for roofs, electrical systems, plumbing systems, driveways, and other capital investments.

Other defects may be far more insidious. Do you notice water damage on the walls in the basement? It's possible that the basement floods once every few years, and while it may look dry now, sooner or later it's going to be full of water. Are those cracks in the foundation the result of a century of settling, or something far more serious? This is where your surveyor's report will be particularly important.

Sometimes the issues cannot be resolved and you may be tempted to take a gamble. Obviously this is a personal choice, but the reward must far outweigh the risks. We have advised clients to walk away from purchases because of insurmountable problems that resisted our best efforts to resolve them. Unless you have an incredibly long term plan, you do not want to acquire a property that will prove problematic to sell later. Remember that the estate agent may be advising that it is not much of a risk, but he/she is the seller's representative. If you want to proceed but your solicitor or surveyor are advising against this, you should seek a second opinion from another specialist in the field.

Most problems can be resolved if handled efficiently. The key is to have a good team in place (see Step 1) and good communication. Throughout the transaction you need to make sure that your solicitor, surveyor and financier are focussed and efficient when handling your purchase.

Proof this works...

"We were very sceptical about incurring the expense of employing a property finder. After we had been looking for a property for a long time, and missed out on several, we finally got sick of it and decided to get some help. Mercury found us a house exactly to the spec that we wanted, which was not yet on the market. It [the transaction] was unbelievably protracted with any number of problems arising which would certainly have led us to walk away from the property if it hadn't been for their help throughout."

– Mr & Mrs Guthrie

Conclusion

Buying a home or property in Prime Central London can be both a dream come true and a very good investment. But if you're not prepared and don't approach the opportunity with deliberate detachment, it's very easy to throw away hundreds of thousands of pounds. You can make a poor purchase, pay too much, or waste money by paying tax unnecessarily or negotiating poorly. In the worst cases you can do all of these – and many people do.

Fortunately most of the steps you need to take to avoid these mistakes are relatively simple. For many they appear too simple or boring to make a difference, which is why most buyers fail to follow them. Consequently they make average or poor acquisitions and fail to put adequate structures in place to protect their wealth.

Admittedly, you'll need to spend some time and energy following these steps, but over the entire process they are guaranteed to save you time, stress and money. You have the choice to follow the boring, disciplined approach that works, or you can try the haphazard approach adopted by most buyers and hope you get lucky. The choice is yours.

Good luck with your search for a property in London! Be thorough, be tough and be fair and you'll find your ideal home while achieving the best terms possible.

A Brief Checklist of the Legal Process

Your solicitor should:
- Receive a memorandum of sale from the estate agents.
- Receive contract papers from the seller's solicitor.
- Raise enquiries and make searches. The searches will vary from environmental to checking if any building projects are planned for the area.
- Receive mortgage offer or confirmation of financing.
- Receive results of enquiries and searches.
- Approve contract (assuming no further enquiries).
- Report on contract to the buyer.
- Receive signed contract and deposit cheque from the buyer and instructions on a completion date (ideally this date will have been set during the negotiations).
- Exchange contracts. This is now a binding agreement to buy and sell and with an agreed completion date (either side can still renege on the deal but not without financial implications).
- The buyer signs the mortgage and the transfer.
- Make post exchange searches, report to financiers, request balance of money from the buyer.
- Complete purchase on contractual completion date (the keys must now be released the the buyer and the property is legally yours).
- Register purchase at HM Land Registry (if necessary).

The process takes approximately six weeks but can be completed in twenty-four hours if both sides agree and are geared to moving that quickly, although some risk is involved in this.

Although these steps seem straightforward, in practice they can be anything but, especially with older buildings which may have been reconfigured over the years. Your solicitor will request evidence of planning permissions, building regulation certificates, proof of building insurance, service charge and ground rent details, to name but a few.

It is essential that you monitor the progress of the legal process. If either party's solicitor is not moving quickly then you need to find out why. If it is your solicitor then that is easily rectified, but if the seller's solicitor appears to be causing delays then you need to speak to the estate agent to rectify the situation.

Unfortunately, the delays may be caused by third parties. Managing agents are notoriously slow at providing details, and the sellers may be disorganised and have lost the insurance details or other salient documents and copies will have to be requested.

Further information

The mystery of the postcodes

A great deal of confusion surrounds the exact deline-
ation of the various areas in prime central London. This
applies to people who are born and bred in London as
well as international buyers. Part of the problem lies in
people's predeliction for confusing the postcodes for
accurate markers for each area. Unfortunately the postcodes were developed by the post office for their use, so
their primary role was to demarcate areas for the ease of
delivery from postal centres. Consequently if someone
says they live in W1 they could live in a mansion on Park
Lane or a flat above a shop in the red light district of
Soho. Below is a brief guide to the postcodes and the
areas they describe:

NW1 – Regent's Park & Primrose Hill – However also
covers Camden.

SW1 – Possibly the most desirable postcode – Bucking-
ham Palace and 10 Downing Street as well as Eaton
Square. It covers Belgravia, parts of Knightsbridge, St
James's, Westminster (SW1P), Victoria and Pimlico
(SW1V).

SW3 – Chelsea and parts of South Kensington and
Knightsbridge, e.g. Egerton Terrace

SW5 – A small zone that is essentially Earl's Court but
also includes the highly desirable Boltons.

SW6 – Fulham & Parson's Green

SW7 – South Kensington & Knightsbridge

SW10 – The western side of Chelsea – Tregunter Road, Cathcart Road, The Ten Acre Estate and then Chelsea Harbour is right on the border with SW6

W1 – A large and diverse area – Mayfair (W1J & W1K), Hanover Square, Regent Street & Savile Row (W1S, W1B), Marylebone & Harley Street (W1H, W1G, W1U), Oxford Street (W1C), Fitzrovia (W1T, W1W), and the slightly racier district of Soho (W1D, W1F).

W2 – North of Hyde Park – Lancaster Gate, Bayswater and Paddington – also Little Venice south of the canal.

W8 – Kensington

W11 – Notting Hill and Holland Park.

W14 – Holland Park and grand villas on Holland Park Villas and Addison Road – does also cover the area west of Holland Road around Kensington Olympia and Brook Green.

Other areas:

NW8 – St John's Wood

NW3 – Hampstead

W9 – Little Venice & Maida Vale

SW11 – covers most of Battersea and the new developments across the river from Chelsea like Montevetro, Albion Riverside.

W6 – Brook Green and Brackenbury Village

Parking

As much of London was built before the car was invented, parking can be an issue. Modern developments tend to provide off street parking and some houses either have garages (often part of a mews house) or off street parking within the boundaries of the property. In every borough one has to apply for a parking permit from the local council. The cost is only a couple of hundred pounds for the year. However, you will only be able to park in a fairly small zone near to your property (with the exception of RBKC where the permit allows you to park in any resident parking space in the entire borough) and you are not guaranteed a space. If you park outside your zone you will need to find a parking meter/metered space or a car park. There is an army of traffic wardens who will issue parking fines or even have your vehicle towed away to a pound. Consequently many of our clients choose to employ chauffeurs.

Important Note: If a building has been converted from office to residential use it is possible that as part of the planning permission the council will refuse the right to parking permits especially if the building is converted into apartments as they do not want added pressure on the shortage of parking spaces. This will be documented so you should check – even if parking is not important to you, it may make it harder to resell the property. This should be reflected in the price and you should negotiate accordingly.

An Overview of Planning Permissions & Building Regulations

If you are planning to acquire a property it is possible that you may want to carry out certain improvements. Although the vendor and estate agent may assure you that you can carry out whatever work you like, this may not be the case. It is essential that you speak to your solicitor so that they can check:

a) That any works that have already been undertaken by past owners conform to the lease as well as the planning restrictions

b) That the work you hope to carry out will be possible.

If it is a standard building then you will probably be able to carry out simple decorations without requiring any planning. However, you cannot take this for granted. For example, most leases in London require the floors to be carpeted rather than for there to be wood floors. The reason for this is the lease will have been written before acoustic soundproofing was even thought possible. Therefore the concern was that the apartment below would suffer whenever you walked on the wood floors in shoes. Obviously technology has improved and in many apartments you can install wooden floors with the freeholder's/landlord's consent as long as suitable soundproofing is used.

This is a very basic example. If you are planning to acquire a property on The Grosvenor estate, in a conservation area or a listed building then you will need consents from various parties to carry out works. In the most extreme cases you will not be able to even repaint a ceiling or remove cornicing. Strangely, however, they may allow you to install a lift in the same building. As you can already tell planning is a complicated issue.

The local planning authority is responsible for granting local planning permission. It can be helpful to informally discuss your development plans with a local planning officer, before putting forward an offer. However, I find that they normally want to see architect's plans before giving an opinion. Even then they are non-commital as they cannot guarantee anything until you have presented a formal application. A much better route is to take an architect or reliable builder to the property before you make an offer (or after you have made an initial low offer).

They will be able to give you a good guide of what is likely to be allowed and what is not. If the work you want to carry out is relatively simple I would just use a reliable builder. You will need to do this anyway so that you can establish the cost of the works as this may impact what you decide to offer for the property. They should also be able to explain the process involved for your particular project. Please note that each council will have their own standards and processes. For example, at the time of writing, the Royal borough of Kensington & Chelsea (RBKC) have implied that they will no longer allow the excavation of "sub-basements" while the City Of Westminster (which includes Belgravia and Mayfair) still seem content to permit suitable excavations.

There Are No Guarantees

Some planning decisions are a mystery to me and I often feel that the planners make questionable decisions merely to justify their existence. It is important to remember that precedents do not have the same weight as they do in the legal system. It is very possible for the property next door to have been granted planning and then for you not to receive it for a similar project – this is especially true for external changes. Therefore if the acquisition hinges on a particularly large alteration that you wish to make it is vital that you speak to an architect who has the contacts and expertise to handle this for you – I cannot state the importance of having an architect and builder who have good contacts with English Heritage, the relevant local council, the relevant estate e.g. Grosvenor. If they have carried out numerous projects in the area they will understand the concerns of each party and what is possible/required to achieve planning permission. These third parties will also trust the architect/builders to do a good job which conforms to their standards, not just aesthetically, but also when considering safety, reduced disturbance to neighbours, the environment, etc.

Although I have painted a fairly unpleasant picture the process is often very smooth. Indeed I have seen lifts installed in Grade 1 listed properties, swimming pools in sub-basements and even added to the ninth floor of an apartment building. However, I wanted to stress the point that you cannot take for granted the fact that you can install wooden floors, remove walls or add ensuite bathrooms just because you have seen it done in other buildings. The chances are that you will be able to, but it is essential to have experts look at the project so that you avoid any unpleasant surprises after you have bought the property.

Glossary

A

Aga – A type of heavy, heat retaining stove. Normally unsuitable for homes in London but some people love them.

Apartment – Also referred to as a flat.

Applicant – Estate agent's term for a buyer (you are not their client).

ARLA – Association of Residential Letting Agents.

Arrangement fees – Fees relating to a specific mortgage product, payable on arrangement of the mortgage.

Asking price – The price of a property on the open market, usually determined by an estate agent.

Auction – A public sale of property, where potential buyers bid against each other to buy the property, with the highest bidder securing the purchase.

B

Bidding war – When two or more parties bid against each other, often leading to sealed bids.

Bijou – Occasionally found in estate agents' details. They are trying to dress up the fact that a property is exceptionally small.

Bridging loan – A short term loan (usually at a higher rate) taken out to cover the financial gap between buying a new property and selling an existing property.

Buildings insurance – An insurance policy to cover against the damage or destruction of the permanent structure of a property.

Buy-to-let – Buying a house or flat with the express intention of letting it out to tenants after the purchase.

C

Cadogan Estate – Owns c. 90 acres of land concentrated around Chelsea, e.g. Cadogan Square.

Capital and interest – A mortgage repayment option whereby the amount borrowed (capital) and the interest accrued are paid back on a monthly basis to the lender.

Capital gains tax – The taxable profit derived from the sale of a capital asset. The capital gain is the difference between the sale price and the basis of the property, after making appropriate adjustments for closing costs, fixing up expenses, capital improvements, allowable depreciation, etc.

Capped rate – Whereby your mortgage interest rate is guaranteed not to rise above an agreed fixed rate for a defined period of period of time.

Caretaker – Normally found in small conversions. Ensures common parts are cleaned and dustbins cleared. Does not offer the same level of service as a porter.

Communal Gardens – Gardens or squares which are not accessible to the public, but are accessible by certain local residents who live on the squares, e.g. Eton Square, Belgrave Square, Ladbroke Square.

Completion – The point at which all transactions concerning the property's sale are concluded and legal transfer of ownership passes to the buyer.

Concierge – Check the services provided! Good ones found in developments such as The Knightsbridge apartments and One Hyde Park. Many developers, however, describe the porter as a "concierge," so you may be disappointed by the service available.

Conservatory – A glass room, usually connected to a house, which is often used as a dining area, playroom, or sitting room.

Contents insurance – Insurance to cover the damage or loss of items and belongings within a property.

Contract – A legal document that details the agreement between buyer and seller that binds both parties to complete the transaction.

Conveyancing – A term to describe the legal work involved in a property transaction that is conducted by a property solicitor.

Cottage – A small house.

Covenants – Agreements written into title deeds which detail an rules or restrictions concerning a particular property.

Credit search – A search most commonly invoked by a lender through a specialised company to ascertain if an individual has CCJs or a bad payment history.

Credit scoring – A numerical value that ranks an individual's credit risk at a given point in time based on a statistical evaluation of information from a credit search.

Cubitt, Thomas – Master builder responsible for much of the architecture in Belgravia and Pimlico.

D

Decking – A raised floor outside of a property, usually in the garden, that is often made of wood.

Demised – Included within the lease or title of the property.

Deeds – A document detailing the ownership of a property, usually held by a mortgage company.

Deposit (for buying a property) – A sum of money (most commonly 10%) paid by the buyer of a property to a mortgage lender upon exchange of contracts.

Deposit (for renting a property) – A sum of money (usually a month's rent in advance) paid to the landlord (or agent) of the property, which is returned at the end of the tenancy, subject to the condition of the property.

Detached – A term used to describe a property that stands alone and is separated from other properties.

Dilapidations – Any disrepair or damage to a rented property.

Disbursements – Fees paid by a solicitor on the buyer's behalf such as Land Registry fees, stamp duty and search fees.

Development – A term used to describe the building of new properties, or the renovation of older properties.

Dormer window – A gabled extension built out from a sloping roof to accommodate a vertical window.

Duplex – An apartment or flat spread over two floors.

E

Eaves – Part of the roof of the building. Often causes restricted head height in loft extensions.

Edwardian – Property from the period when Edward VII was king of England (1901-1910).

Elizabethan – Property from the period when Queen Elizabeth I was the ruler of England (1558-1603).

Enfranchiseable – A lease which qualifies for a lease extension.

End of terrace – A house situated at the end of a row of terraced houses.

English Heritage – An organization, partly funded by government aid, that looks after ancient monuments and historic buildings in England. The official name is The Historic Buildings and Monuments Commission for England.

En Suite – A bedroom constructed with its own toilet and bathroom (i.e. it does not share these facilities with any room).

E.P.C. – Energy Performance Certificate.

Equity release – A means of retaining the use of your house or other object which has capital value, while also obtaining a steady stream of income, using the value of the house.

Estate agent – A business that arranges the selling, renting (letting agents), or management of homes, land and other buildings (property management agents).

Exchange of contracts – When contracts are exchanged between the buyer's and seller's solicitors, legally committing both parties to the sale/purchase of the property at the agreed price.

Exclusivity clause – Gives you sole right to buy the property for a defined period of time. However, this can be difficult to enforce legally as either side can delay the transaction until the period has lapsed.

F

Fixed rate mortgage – Where the interest rate on a mortgage is fixed for a set period of time, meaning monthly repayments are unaffected by upward or downward movements in the standard variable rate.

Flat – See apartment.

Flexible mortgage – A mortgage product that offers the borrower the flexibility to overpay or underpay on their mortgage in a given month.

Floorplan – The layout of a property showing the dimensions and spatial relationships between rooms, entrances, etc. These can vary in size for the same property depending on the company.

Freehold – The ownership of a property, meaning that it belongs to the owner without the limitation of time.

G

Garage – A building where a car is kept, which is built next to, or as part of, a house.

Gazumping – When a seller accepts a higher offer from a third party on a property that they have already agreed to sell to another party, but have not yet exchanged contracts.

Gazundering – When a buyer offers the seller a lower offer than the previously agreed selling price just before contracts are about to be exchanged.

Georgian – Belonging to the period when Kings Georges I, II, and III ruled Britain, especially from 1714 to 1811.

Ground rent – An annual charge levied by the freeholder to the leaseholder.

Grosvenor Estate – Owns much of Belgravia and Mayfair.

Guarantor – An individual who offers to be contractually liable, both financially and legally, should a tenant fail to pay the rent during their tenancy, or in the event of damage to the property.

Guide price – An indication of the price that the property is expected to sell for and what the vendor is hoping to achieve.

H

HMO – House in multiple occupation.

Home Information Packs (HIPs) – A series of documents (including an Energy Performance Certificate) recently introduced by the UK government to speed up the home buying and selling process and also to save consumers money on house sales and purchases which, for one reason or another may not complete.

House – A building in which people, usually one family, live.

House boat – A boat which people use as their home, normally situated on a river bank or canal, e.g. Chelsea Embankment and Little Venice.

Howard de Walden estate – The "medical district" near Harley Street. The Howard de Walden Estate is owned directly and indirectly by a number of members of the Howard de Walden Family. The Estate owns, manages and leases the majority of the ninety-two acres of real estate within Marylebone, which comprises the area from Marylebone High Street in the west to Robert Adam's Portland Place in the east and from Wigmore Street in the south to Marylebone Road in the north.

I

IFA – Independent Financial Adviser.

Inheritance tax – A tax paid to the government based on wealth (money, property, etc.) passed from one person to another during their lifetime or as part of their estate after death. Also know as IHT.

Insurance – An agreement in which you pay a company a recurring fee and they pay your costs if you have an accident, injury, etc., or if your property or possessions are damaged or lost.

Instruction – The term estate agents use to describe a property, e.g. a new instruction = a new property (as they have been "instructed" to sell the property

Interest – Money that is charged by a bank or other financial organisation for borrowing money. Calculated as a percentage of the amount borrowed.

Interest-only mortgage – A mortgage repayment option, whereby the borrower only repays the lender the interest on the amount borrowed. The borrower must still pay back the capital, or amount borrowed (usually through an investment vehicle).

Inventory – A list detailing every item contained within a rental property and the condition each listed item is in, usually checked by all parties on the day the tenant moves in and signed by all parties.

J

Joint sole agency – The use of more than one estate agent to sell your property simultaneously.

K

Knotweed, Japanese – Virulent strain of plant that can case sever damage. Many mortgage lenders will refuse finance if this plant is discovered in the survey. However, it can be removed by specialists (simply cutting and burning the plant is insufficient)

L

Land Registry – A government body that maintains and updates records of land ownership and property ownership.

Lateral – Should only be used to describe an apartment on one floor. However, estate agents will use it to describe anything that is wider than normal! E.g. "a lateral house on four floors."

Law Society – The representative body for solicitors in England and Wales. Ensure that your solicitor is a member.

Lease – A legal document by which the freehold (or leasehold) owner of a property lets the premises or a part of it to another party for a specified length of time, after the expiry of which, ownership may revert to the freeholder or superior leaseholder.

Leasehold – A legally binding document whereby the freeholder grants the right for the leaseholder to possess, or the use of land or a building for a specific period of time.

Lender – Usually a business, such as a bank or building society from whom one borrows money, or to whom one owes money.

Letting – When a property owner leases or rents out a property to tenants.

Letting agent – A business that arranges the letting or management of homes rented on behalf of private and corporate individuals.

Lifetime mortgage – A form of equity release, whereby one can borrow an amount of money against part of, or all, the value of your home, and interest is charged on the amount you borrow.

Lightwell – Allows some light into the centre of large buildings. Often ugly and poorly maintained due to difficult access. Unfortunately it's the only natural light for some bedrooms in older mansion blocks, e.g. Mayfair.

Listed building – A building of great historical or artistic value, which has official protection to prevent it from being changed or destroyed.

Loan to value – The amount of a mortgage relative to the property's value.

Local authority search – When a solicitor makes an enquiry to the land registry to ascertain if there are any future development issues or outstanding enforcements that might affect a property or surrounding area, which might influence the decision to purchase the property.

Loft – A space at the top of a building, under the roof, used for storage, or sometimes converted into a room.

Lower ground floor – The estate agents' euphemism for a basement flat. Sometimes also referred to as the garden level. May have direct access to the garden or alley behind the building.

M

Maisonette – A property arranged over more than one floor, usually as part of an existing house.

Managing/management agent – A third party business that manages the letting of properties, in exchange for a fee, on behalf of a landlord or property owner.

Mansard roof – A mansard or mansard roof (also called a French roof) is a four-sided gambrel-style hip roof characterized by two slopes on each of its sides with the lower slope, punctured by dormer windows, at a steeper angle than the upper. The roof creates an additional floor of habitable space, such as a garret. The upper slope of the roof may not be visible from street level when viewed from close proximity to the building.

Mansion – A very large and expensive house.

Mews house – A building which was used in the past for keeping horses and is now used as a house.

Mews (street) – A short narrow road containing mews houses.

Mezzanine – A small additional floor between one floor of a building and the next floor up. Many apartments have been ruined by trying to add mezzanine levels to create extra square feet instead of keeping the fantastic double height rooms. One reason why pound-per-square-foot comparisons do not always work.

Mid-terraced house – A house situated within a terrace with a house attached on either side.

Mortgage deeds – A legal document detailing a lender's interest in a property along with the terms of the mortgage.

Mortgage – An agreement which allows you to borrow money from a bank or lender in order to buy a property.

Mortgagee – A bank, or similar organisation, which provides mortgages to people especially so that they can buy a property.

N

NAEA – National Association of Estate Agents.

Negative equity – When the value of a property is less than the value of the mortgage outstanding on a property. Also called being "underwater."

New-build – A house or flat that has been built from scratch by a building company or developer to be sold on.

NHBC – National House-Builders Council.

Non-refundable deposit – A deposit used in exchange for a guarantee that the seller will not market the property once an agreement has been reached. A risky strategy, as the sellers may not own the property in its entirety or there may be serious structural issues.

O

Offer price – The financial offer a prospective buyer submits to the estate agent as a price they are willing to pay for a property.

Off-plan – The purchase of a property before the building work itself has started, or has been completed.

Ombudsman – Independent professional bodies that deal with complaints by consumers made about particular organisations, such as estate agents. (Ombudsman of Estate Agents).

Open day – When a property is opened up to prospective buyers to view over a set period of time to increase the competitiveness of a property sale.

OSP – Off-street parking.

P

Patio – An area outside a house with a solid floor but no roof that is used especially for eating, or in good weather.

Penthouse – A luxurious apartment, or set of rooms, at the top of a hotel or tall block.

Period property – Estate agent jargon; obviously every property comes from a certain period. Estate agents use the term to describe older properties.

Planning permission – Formal approval provided by a local planning authority, or council, often with conditions, allowing a planned development to proceed.

Plot – A piece of land that has been marked, or measured, for an individual house or flat to be built, or an individual property unit within a wider new property development.

P.O.A. (price on application) – Usually for very expensive properties, the asking price is not advertised within the public domain and is only obtainable through the estate agent.

Pounds per square foot – The price per square foot of a property. Beware, as this can be a very misleading figure (see mezzanine).

Portman Estate – Owns c. one hundred acres north of Oxford Street, e.g. Portman Square.

Property search agent/property finder – A company that will find and arrange viewings for particular properties to buy or rent matching your search criteria on your behalf.

Q

Quirky – The estate agents' way of saying "poorly configured."

R

Rebuilding cost – The cost of fully rebuilding a property, usually requested as part of a buildings insurance policy.

Recycling – When paper, glass, plastic, etc. is processed so that it can be used again.

Redemption – When a mortgage is paid off in full.

Renovation – The process of repairing and/or improving a property.

Repayment mortgage – A mortgage where monthly repayments include both the capital and interest components, meaning at the end of the term, the mortgage will be paid off in full.

Repossession – When a mortgage company takes possession of a property, primarily due to non-payment of a mortgage.

Rent – A fixed amount of money that you pay regularly to the owner of a property for the uninterrupted use and enjoyment of it for an agreed period of time.

Retention – The process of withholding money from a seller until certain improvements or corrections to the property have been completed to satisfaction.

RICS – Royal Institute of Chartered Surveyors. Ensure that your building surveyor is a member.

S

Sealed bid – Where interested parties send a confidential letter detailing the amount they are willing to pay for a property (to buy or rent). The highest bidder usually secures the property.

Searches – A request for any information concerning a particular property, usually held by a local authority or the Land Registry.

Semi-detached – A property that is joined to another house on one side.

Service charge – A charge to cover the cost of repairing and maintaining external or internal communal parts of a building, usually paid by the tenant or leaseholder.

Serviced apartments – Self-contained apartments designed to provide general amenities for short stays.

Share of freehold – Form of tenure. The property will have a lease but also a share in the company that owns the freehold.

Sole agent – When only one estate agent is instructed to sell or let a property.

Solicitor – Legal expert who handles all of the documents relating to the purchase or sale of a property.

Stamp Duty Land Tax (SDLT) – A tax property buyers pay to the government, the value of which depends on the value of the property being bought (ranging between 1% and 4% of the purchase price).

Store room – Separate from main apartment. Small area normally in basement to store bikes and luggage. Check to see that it is not included in total square feet, as obviously this is worth less.

Structural survey – A detailed assessment of a property's structure, designed to highlight faults or defects that might impact upon its value of the property.

Stucco – Fine plaster used for coating wall surfaces normally painted white. Especially prevalent in Belgravia; hence, "White Stucco Fronted House."

Studio flat – A flat with one main room, or open-plan living area, that usually incorporates cooking facilities with a separate bathroom.

Sub-basement – Sometimes described as a "lower, lower ground floor." Often recently excavated to provide room for a swimming pool, gym, media room or other room that does not require natural light.

Subject to contract – A term meaning that an agreement for buying a property has been reached, but will not be legally binding until after the exchange of contracts.

Standard variable rate (SVR) – The basic interest rate offered by a mortgage lender that may increase or decrease at the lender's discretion.

T

Tenancy agreement – A contract between a tenant and a landlord that specifies certain rights and obligations for both parties for the duration of the tenancy.

Tenant – A person who has a temporary right to possess a property.

Tenure – Refers to the status of a property, usually in terms of whether it is leasehold or freehold.

Terraced house – A property that is part of a group of connected houses.

Thatched roof – A roof made of tightly bundled or woven straw or reeds.

Timeshare – A holiday house or apartment that is jointly owned by several different people, each of whom is able to use it for a particular period of the year.

Title deeds – Documents displaying the legal owner of a property.

Townhouse – A house in a town or city, usually a comfortable, expensive one in a fashionable area.

Transfer deed – A document from the Land Registry highlighting the transfers in legal ownership of a property from a seller to a buyer.

Tube affected – A property that is located above or near to an underground train tunnel/track. Therefore some noise, and in worst cases the entire building can shake, e.g. Moore Street in Chelsea.

U

Under offer – A term indicating the status of a property after an offer from a buyer has been accepted, but before contracts have been exchanged.

V

Vacant possession – Unless you are taking over a tenant you will want vacant possession. This also protects you if squatters invade the property between exchange and completion as it will be the sellers' responsibility.

Valuation – The process of understanding a property's value, usually conducted by either a surveyor or an estate agent.

Vendor – The technical name for someone selling a property.

Victorian – A property built during the time when Queen Victoria was Queen of Britain (1837-1901).

Villa – A larger, detached home with grounds.

Void – The period in which a property lies empty in between periods of tenant occupation.

W

Warehouse – A large building for storing items before they are sold.

Wet room – A waterproof room that contains a shower but no cubicle/shower area. Normally used in small apartments where space is at a premium.

Wide angle lens – Used to make rooms look bigger and grander in estate agents' details.

X

Xcruciating – The spelling and grammar in estate agents' details, e.g. "highly sort-after property."

Y

Yield – Income generated from a property relative to the value of the property.

Z

Zoopla – the bizarre name of a property website.

About The Author

Jeremy McGivern was educated at Eton College. The entrepreneurial spirit comes from both of his parents: his father was an entrepreneur with several businesses and his mother was a highly successful business woman who helped a number of "start-up companies". In 2001 Jeremy founded Mercury Homesearch and has since become the leading expert on acquiring property in prime central London. He has featured in and written articles for Bloomberg Television, The Financial Times, Money Week, The Daily Telegraph, Spear's Wealth Management Survey and The Sunday Times to name but a few.

He is married to Serena and has two children, Milo & Flora. He also has seven Godchildren: Charlie in Australia, Isabel in Dubai. In the U.K. – Xander, Louis, Amelia, Sam, and Theo.

Outside of property, sport is his great passion. He says: "Tragically my eagerness is not matched by talent. Age has also caught up with me so I am now only able to play football sporadically. I still play squash and golf regularly and run the occasional marathon." He actively raises money for Leukaemia Research, The Eve Appeal and The Sarah Matheson Trust.

Notes

Lightning Source UK Ltd.
Milton Keynes UK
UKOW06f2205050915

258089UK00013B/100/P